# Design and Build a Cross-Country Course

# Endorsements

*I have read Hugh Morshead's book with great interest and enjoyment. He has managed to combine clarity of expression with a real depth of insight, and I believe the book will be an extremely useful guide for designers and course builders at all levels, but especially those who do not yet have vast experience.*

*I had the good fortune to work with Hugh Morshead when he first started course building in the USA and I am delighted he has made a success of his career. If his book inspires just one new designer or builder to 'have a go', then the effort he has put into writing it will be well rewarded.*

HUGH THOMAS

*Fantastically interesting book. Having ridden over many cross-country courses, I had no idea of the care, worry and knowledge it takes to make a top course builder. I have learned so much, not only about fence design, but also about terrain and management. With wonderful amusing moments, Hugh has written a winner.*

GINNY ELLIOT

*I very much enjoyed reading this book and thought it was written in a user-friendly and cheerful way. For competitors, organisers and course builders/designers alike, it should be a 'must' on their coffee table as a quick and helpful reference.*

IAN STARK

# Design and Build a Cross-Country Course

**second edition**

## HUGH MORSHEAD

KENILWORTH PRESS

Copyright © 2005 Hugh Morshead

First published in the UK in 2005
by Kenilworth Press, an imprint of Quiller Publishing Ltd

This edition published 2011

**British Library Cataloguing-in-Publication Data**
A catalogue record for this book
is available from the British Library

ISBN 978 1 905693 35 1

The right of Hugh Morshead to be identified as the author of this work has been asserted in accordance with the Copyright, Design and Patent Act 1988

The information in this book is true and complete to the best of our knowledge. All recommendations are made without any guarantee on the part of the Publisher, who also disclaims any liability incurred in connection with the use of this data or specific details.

All rights reserved. No part of this book may be reproduced or transmitted in any form or by any means, electronic or mechanical including photocopying, recording or by any information storage and retrieval system, without permission from the Publisher in writing.

Design by Paul Saunders
Fence diagrams by Sally Bostock
Layout by Kenilworth Press
Printed in Singapore by KHL Printing Co Pte Ltd

KENILWORTH PRESS
An imprint of Quiller Publishing Ltd
Wykey House, Wykey, Shrewsbury, SY4 1JA
Tel: 01939 261616 Fax: 01939 261606
E-mail: info@quillerbooks.com
Website: www.kenilworthpress.co.uk

## Disclaimer

This book is written in the spirit of sharing knowledge and experience. The publisher and author disclaim any responsibility or liability for any loss or injury that may occur as a result of the information, procedures or techniques contained in this book.

# Contents

| | | |
|---|---|---|
| Acknowledgements | | 6 |
| Foreword by Captain Mark Phillips | | 7 |
| Introduction (2011) | | 8 |
| Chapter 1 | Reading the Land | 11 |
| Chapter 2 | Designing the Course | 14 |
| Chapter 3 | Cost-Effective Design | 18 |
| Chapter 4 | Fences That Don't Work | 22 |
| Chapter 5 | Footing | 29 |
| Chapter 6 | Striding | 34 |
| Chapter 7 | Portable Fences | 37 |
| Chapter 8 | Mainstay Fences | 50 |
| Chapter 9 | Combinations | 95 |
| Chapter 10 | Banks and Steps | 111 |
| Chapter 11 | Water Jumps | 125 |
| Chapter 12 | Construction Techniques and Tricks of the Trade | 136 |
| Chapter 13 | Pony Club Course Building | 151 |
| Chapter 14 | Short Course Eventing, Hunter Trials and Team Chasing | 160 |
| Chapter 15 | Cross-Country Fences for Training Centres | 165 |
| Chapter 16 | Land Management | 167 |
| Chapter 17 | Risk Assessment and Crisis Management | 171 |
| Chapter 18 | Falling with Style | 175 |
| Glossary | | 177 |
| Appendix A: Guidelines for Short Course Eventing | | 179 |
| Appendix B: Horse Trials Organiser's Master Plan | | 181 |
| Appendix C: Imperial and Metric Conversions | | 183 |
| Appendix D: Timber | | 184 |
| Appendix E: Fence by Fence Materials List | | 188 |
| Index | | 191 |

# Acknowledgements

This book grew over time and many people generously gave their advice, encouragement and support.

I am deeply indebted to Capt Mark Phillips for writing the foreword, and to Ginny Elliot, Hugh Thomas and Ian Stark for their endorsements – thank you.

My grateful thanks to the following for reading the manuscript and also for their comments and suggestions: Judy Hodgkinson, Ian Roberts, Kelly Plitz, Martha Griggs, Susan Laing, Momo Lafromboise, and Anne and Claus Zander.

My special thanks to Sally Bostock for the care and effort she devoted to the illustrations, and to Charlotte Harper and Claus Zander for the photographs.

I am also beholden to Russell Smith, Sue Collins and Nicole and Alan Shinton for their contributions.

I would like gratefully to acknowledge the enthusiasm and patience of Lesley Gowers and David Blunt both previously of Kenilworth Press.

My greatest debt and thanks go to my loving wife Caroline for her support and encouragement, and to my sons, Christopher and James, for giving me a lead when my computer needed coaxing.

To all these kind people, and to many others, who have helped make this book possible I am most grateful. Any errors or omissions are mine alone.

Finally, this book is dedicated to my parents who filled Lucy, Sam and me with the spirit of the chase and to all the horses who made it possible.

# Foreword

I was lucky enough to get to know and work with Hugh Morshead more than twenty years ago while working on cross-country courses in North America.

Working with him was a real pleasure, not just because of his ability to build fences but also because of his insight into how a horse reacts and thinks in different circumstances. This is not something that is easily taught but rather an instinct and a feeling gained from a lifetime with horses.

It is no accident that Ireland produces so many great horses and horsemen. The hunting field and racecourses on the Emerald Isle are a unique learning environment for all those lucky enough to experience it. Hugh has drawn on all his experiences when compiling this book.

These pages truly reflect course design and course building from a horseman's perspective.

CAPTAIN MARK PHILLIPS

# Introduction (2011)

## Notes on changes in the sport since first publication

THERE HAVE BEEN MANY CHANGES IN EVENTING since this book was published in 2005, perhaps more in the past decade than in the history of the sport. The amount of change combined with other uncertainties can be unsettling, however, take a long view and a reassuring pattern emerges. Like an echo from the past, horsemanship and land stewardship remain essential to success.

Baby boomers drive the juggernaut of change. They took an amateur sport and with their numbers and cash gave it a professional ambience. The backdrop has also changed; society is now more urban and egalitarian in nature. Today many riders grow up without the rough and tumble of Pony Club and the hunt field. The recent past was a time of great courses and riding; it went almost unnoticed that technical skill had outpaced horsemanship – then came the falls.

The number and apparent randomness of the fatalities shook Eventing to the core. The response was a sea change in how the sport is run. In the past, knowledge and leadership was dominated by individuals who had dedicated their lives to the horse. While generous with their wisdom, course builders and others had to be peripatetic to learn their craft. Today, under FEI leadership, there is consensus on every facet of the sport. Not only are guidelines and directives available for all on their website, but research and data collecting is on going. Horse shows are as much about people as they are about horses, but there is a recognition that the key to success is to design from a horse's viewpoint.

Competitions depend upon good weather and generous sponsors. In the past, keeping the fingers crossed and making a few quick phone calls did the job. Plan B was the wellies, the Barbour and an air of desperation on the phone to loosen the purse strings. Those days are gone and with the economy and the weather swinging on their hinges, both these issues need to be tackled head-on. There are many ways to mitigate the effects of drought and flood. Essentially it comes down to land stewardship and working with nature. Understanding soil dynamics and storm water management is an important part of course design. Both require long-term planning and capital outlay. The results are improved footing and a broader range of conditions under which a competition can successfully run. It also makes economic sense.

Horse shows have become flower shows and I am nonplussed when cleaning up after a show I have to dump tubs of wilting chrysanthemums into the dumpster when so much time has been wasted in the hunt for logs. Natural landscaping is easy on the eye, the budget and can save the course builder from grief. Often in the rush to meet a deadline, the once pristine site can appear to the organiser slightly trashed. It is a simple job to rearrange boulders, add a splash of mulch and plant perennials. A perceived calamity then becomes landscaping that chimes with the jumps.

Other disasters are more serious. Safety is paramount and it is imperative to do everything possible to reduce falls. Enlightened course design goes a long way in preventing disaster, while building deformable jumps can reduce the severity of injuries. Currently the two main ways to have a deformable fence are with brush or frangible pins. Installing frangible pins is relatively straightforward; however, hands-on instruction is necessary as their effectiveness can be reduced by up to 40% if improperly installed. Brush jumps come in many forms and it is hard to beat them for price or aesthetic appeal.

Many of the other changes are about clarity; for example, revetting is capped with a half-round so that it is clearly defined and the revetting out of water may have a flower box at its base so that horses jump clean. The trend is to build water jumps without revetting if feasible. There have been problems jumping out over revetting; the splash may be a factor or simply the range of horses striding through water.

Building water jumps without revetting can reduce construction costs by a third. Construction techniques have also changed. Coping with the vagaries of the weather, the water table and machinery in mud can take the poetry out of course building. Today it is easier to site water jumps in the optimum location because they only need a few inches of water and do not require revetting. Impermeable liners are available in many grades. It is not necessary to use the same quality as that required for tailing ponds. Similarly, it is not necessary for the base to have multiple grades of rock and gravel. Nine inches of crushed limestone screenings will make a reliable and long lasting base. The best way to pack it is with water. Cover the screening with water, then drain the water and allow the screening to completely dry. Repeat the process three times and the footing will set firm. Screening is soft because of the air trapped between the grains. Water forces the air out, drying consolidates the footing. This is a far more efficient method than using a packer. The water jump must be sited with natural drainage so that the capped pipe at the base can be used to drain the water.

The sport continues to evolve, however the core principles of design and traditional jump building endure. Those principles include: siting jumps off a turn and on rising ground so that the horse is naturally in a frame conducive to jumping and using brush and ditches to give the perception of challenge. It all comes down to building from a horse's viewpoint – the spectator may see obstacles but the horse sees jumps and that is what this book is all about.

Hugh Morshead, 2011

# 1.

# Reading the Land

READING THE LAND is how the designer dovetails the competition requirements to the terrain, without having to tear the skin off the land with bulldozers. The first step is to have an appreciation of the requirements of the riders, coaches and grooms. Look after them; they are your customers.

When looking at the site, think of a clock. For horse trials the three big cogs are dressage, show jumping and cross-country. The parking area and warm-up rings are smaller cogs, and then there are the multitude of tiny wheels and springs that make it all tick. Some parts may appear insignificant, but for a smooth operation the tiniest spring is as important as the biggest cog. This analogy applies to personnel, as well as to the physical qualities of a competition.

Horse trials can be frantic, desperate affairs. The site plan should make it as easy as possible for all the players. Warm-up rings and lorry parking should be in close proximity. This enables coaches and riders with multiple entries to be as time-efficient as possible. The ideal site plan is a cloverleaf shape. The three disciplines are represented by the leaves and the warm-up areas are close to the point where the leaves join the stem.

Good footing on the cross-country course is imperative. The fences will get all the attention, but they could be 'virtual reality'. It is the track surface that the horses come in contact with, and this can do immediate and long-term damage to tendons and ligaments. The footing has to stand up not only to the wear and

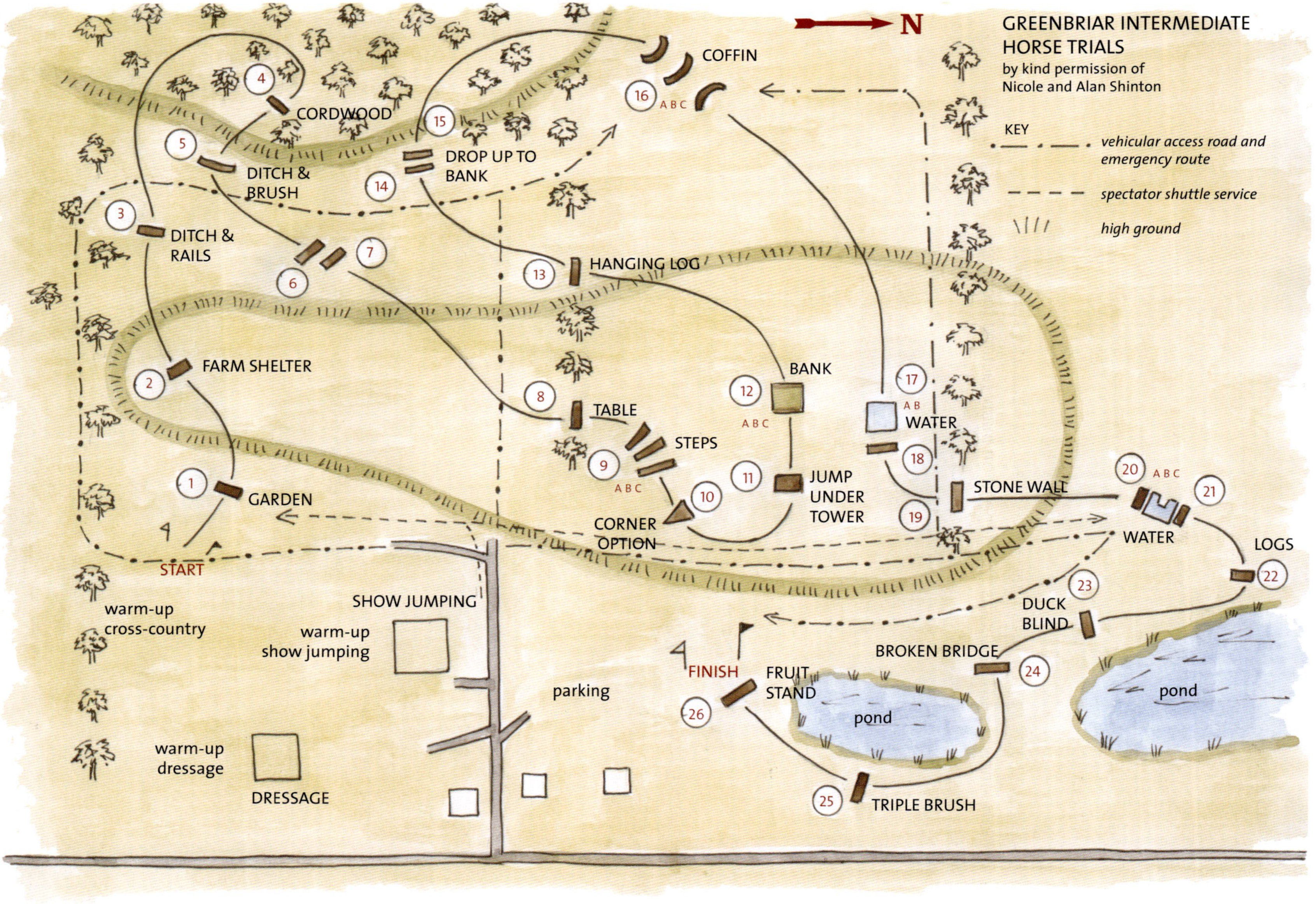
GREENBRIAR INTERMEDIATE
HORSE TRIALS
by kind permission of
Nicole and Alan Shinton
KEY
vehicular access road and
emergency route
spectator shuttle service
high ground
N
START
1
GARDEN
2
FARM SHELTER
3
DITCH &
RAILS
4
CORDWOOD
5
DITCH &
BRUSH
6
7
8
TABLE
9
A B C
STEPS
10
CORNER
OPTION
11
JUMP
UNDER
TOWER
12
A B C
BANK
13
HANGING LOG
14
15
DROP UP TO
BANK
16
A B C
COFFIN
17
A B
WATER
18
19
STONE WALL
20
A B C
21
WATER
22
LOGS
23
DUCK
BLIND
24
BROKEN BRIDGE
25
TRIPLE BRUSH
26
FRUIT
STAND
FINISH
pond
pond
parking
SHOW JUMPING
warm-up
show jumping
warm-up
cross-country
warm-up
dressage
DRESSAGE

tear of horses, vehicles and pedestrians, but also the vagaries of the weather. Too often courses are built and the footing is an afterthought, when time and cash have long since dribbled away.

The first step is to walk the site thoroughly and note all the natural and man-made features, such as, roads, fence lines, streams and the lie of the land. The location of the start and finish, the potential water jump site and other feature fences will be the first to fall into place. A rough outline of the course will now be taking shape. The details will depend on many factors: footing, vehicular access and camber are all major concerns.

Camber is the key to a course that will ride with balance and rhythm. This term describes a track surface that is slightly convex, such as a banked turn on a racetrack. Negative camber describes ground that slopes away on a turn, and this is prone to being slippery. A horse falling on the flat is a serious design flaw. Taking full advantage of the natural dips and slopes can prevent this. The slow process of soil-creep results in better turf on the lower slopes, and these can also provide a positive camber for wide, swinging turns. The higher ground of ridges is advantageous in wet weather and improves visibility for spectators. It does make a big difference if as many fences as possible can be seen from a central location.

Landowners and farm managers may encourage you to use existing tracks through woodland. Avoid the lure of the woods. They do provide variety, but the footing problems associated with slippery wet leaves, exposed roots and fragile leaf mould are expensive to fix and would never be accepted if encountered on open terrain.

It is easy to get excited about all the natural features that a site has to offer. However, generally less is more. It is best to keep the course uncomplicated for the first year and increase the challenge over time.

All fences must be accessible to vehicles and this includes a two-wheel drive ambulance. Nothing destroys footing quite as quickly as regular use by trucks, animals and pedestrians. The access routes to the fences needs to be carefully thought out, so that emergency vehicles, spectators and competitors do not have to share the same track.

# 2.

# Designing the Course

*'Checkin' the crazy ones*
*Coaxin' the unaisy ones*
*An' liftin' the lazy ones*
*On with a stick'*

THESE LINES FROM A TRADITIONAL IRISH BALLAD could be about the challenges facing the course designer. Standards have to be maintained, the range of competitors' abilities assessed, and the interests of sponsors, officials and organisers all balanced. All the players come with their own agendas, and these are not always compatible. It is worth having a look at these different concerns.

Riders expect a fair challenge, but a championship will obviously be more demanding. Sponsors want to boost prestige and sales. Officials, like stockbrokers, consider a quiet day as a good day. Course builders appreciate practicality, and the organiser should be able to glow in the radiant warmth of altruism.

To be successful, competitors must ride with authority. The same holds true for designers. The ability to design comes from accumulated experience and over time, making the right decision becomes intuitive.

Horsemanship and common sense are recognised as essential skills, which of course they are. But I believe that being assertive is equally indispensable. This means having the ability to say no and let your judgement and intuition be your guide. When asked to work on an existing course, some course builders may err on the side of diplomacy. I consider it a mandate for change.

It is imperative for the smooth operation of the sport that cross-country courses have the appropriate level of difficulty and show consistency from year to year. There may be extenuating circumstances, such as wet conditions or a show in an isolated area may be a shade kinder than the national average.

Nevertheless, it is the designer's responsibility to ensure that courses meet national standards at the lower levels and international standards at the upper levels. If this is not done, riders and horses may be upgraded too quickly, which can result in problems when they tackle a course that is up to the mark.

It is difficult, but necessary, to keep up with all the rule changes. Fences are built to last for at least five, if not ten years. It helps to be able to anticipate the expected changes. This can prevent organisers and technical delegates from having cross words. The rules must be followed implicitly, both in letter and spirit. This is not always as straightforward as it appears. Many of the rules regarding cross-country courses are subjective in nature. When a course designer is asked to give new life and ideas to an existing course, a difference of opinion and interpretation of the rules can be expected. It is only fair to warn the organiser in advance, which fences can stay and which must go.

Designing the course so that it is the correct distance is an obvious, but critical part of the design process. I doubt that there is a simpler task in which errors are made more frequently. The course must be wheeled from start to finish before and after the course is built. The route that is wheeled must be the optimum track for the average competitor.

As you walk the site, the course should be falling into place like a jigsaw puzzle. The second step turns a potential collection of seemly unrelated fences into a competition, offering horse and rider a fair challenge over a series of obstacles that ebb and flow with rhythm and reason. This is the essence of course design and it is a blend of educating, testing and providing good old-fashioned sport. A good cross-country course is a test of horsemanship and should ask the following questions: the training of horse and rider and the communication between them, boldness, carefulness, good judgement, balance and athletic ability.

Proficient course designers know intuitively what type of fence goes where. For the less experienced there is a framework, which, when used with common sense, can be applied to any competition. The first three fences should encourage horses and get a rhythm established. Riding with determination is easier if they are built on rising ground. Each of these fences can be progressively more challenging. For example, ascending rails, roll-top farm shelter to parallel rails. By the fifth fence, that racecourse reject may be having such a good time that he has momentarily forgotten his age and arthritis and is tearing up the ground at full stretch. Designers can do much to encourage control and penalise wild riding. At the lower levels a simple turning question of ascending rails set at right angles with three or four strides between them will make competitors steady up. Downhill steps to convex rails will achieve the same at the upper levels.

The terrain should decide the nature and location of the combinations. Although there should be a natural progression of challenges, this does not mean that the course gets increasingly more difficult. But rather, each fence sets competitors up for the next. For example, if an imposing trakehner is planned, then consider having an inviting ditch and brush earlier on the course. The trakehner can now be ridden with hope and confidence.

Filler fences such as barrels, cordwoods or farm shelters seldom rate a second glance. From a horse's point of view they are essential. They give confidence, are instrumental in establishing a rhythm, and encourage horses and riders to have a bold, galloping cross-country style of riding. It is better to have several of these types of fences in a row, rather than alternating between straightforward and difficult fences. These uncomplicated fences are usually built close to maximum dimensions.

Options and alternative routes are how the designer gives the winning edge to the best and keeps the less experienced in the game. An option is an easier, slower route. Alternative routes are approximately equal in difficulty, but give riders a choice of routes. For example, one route will suit the short-coupled, handy athletic type, while the other is better for the big-striding bold jumper. Using options to justify an inappropriately huge fence is not in the spirit of the sport. Horses and riders are for the most part a known quantity at the upper levels of competition. As the jumps get smaller the unpredictability rises and you have to anticipate the tired, inexperienced and poorly ridden horse.

The weather is the other great unknown and the course should be designed so that it can easily be modified at the last minute. A selection of portable fences facilitates this.

The final two or three fences do a similar job to the ones at the beginning of the course and enable riders to finish on a good note. However, they should not be so easy that competitors stop riding.

Course design is learned with the boots on, rather than the books open. Every site is unique and deserves its own design. The sport evolves and grows through the cross-pollination of ideas; the trick is in knowing which ideas to germinate. It is far better to have a grasp of the fundamentals, rather than a grab-bag of jump ideas. The enlightened course designer paints with big logs a flowing picture on the landscape like the bold broad brush stokes of Chinese calligraphy.

## CHAPTER 2 | DESIGNING THE COURSE

The principles of design are:

- Maintain the standard and follow the rules.
- Keep it simple.
- Fit the course to the terrain.
- Use fences and terrain to set horses up.
- Anticipate the tired, inexperienced and poorly ridden horses.
- Organisers need to work together so that one competition sets horses up for the next.
- Restrain your imagination and think like a horse.

# 3.

# Cost-Effective Design

Successful horse trials have more to do with the skills and management of the people involved, than the size of the budget or the scenic qualities of the site. The good news for budget-minded organisers is that there are ways to build courses for considerably less than expected, without compromising standards or safety. The bad news is that building the course is the easy part. The quality of the show is defined by the organisation running the competition.

Just as the trick to riding winners on the racecourse is to get the ride on the horse that is going to win, it is prudent for designers and builders to assess the organiser's ability to run a successful show. To be cost-effective is sound business sense. But, if it is just the face of parsimony, then there are real safety concerns about the operation and course maintenance from year to year. Even the most professionally built courses will require maintenance and a thorough inspection prior to each competition. These costs have to be included in the budget.

Organisers also need to keep their eyes open when hiring course designers and builders. As that adage from the backstretch reminds us – horses are second only to religion in providing opportunities for the unscrupulous to make money from the gullible. Course designers and builders write their reputations across the countryside with telegraph poles and railway sleepers (ties). However, there are at least three operating styles that can cause regret:

**Happy Harry's Honour System.** This refers to posts that are barely in the ground and the jumps are on their honour not to collapse until the first horse is on course. The repair crew can then take care of them.

**Michelangelo's Prodigy**. The fences are all magnificently built and finished. But do you want to pay for artwork, when all you need is a jump?

**Paint-by-Numbers Course Design**. This is when an impressive album of photographs of prestigious courses is used to reproduce another course, regardless of terrain or the level of competition. *Caveat imitator*.

Good planning is essential. The first step for the organiser is to get the designer, builder and farm manager to walk the site together and discuss every aspect of the project. This meeting can at least identify the challenges – the designer's latent edifice complex, the builder juggling an impossible schedule and the farm manager tottering toward a sense of humour failure. However, all three do agree that they can detect no pulse of logic in the organiser.

The next step can also be a challenge. The design plans and the construction materials have to be on the site the day the course building begins. This is not as simple as it sounds. Designers are reluctant to draw up detailed plans until the dense jungle of briars and underbrush has been cleared.

The organiser is hesitant to empty the bank account to buy construction materials that may not meet with the builder's approval. The answer is to have on hand at least two weeks' supply of construction materials on site and sufficient design plans. It is an expensive mistake to ask the course builder to log timber off the property. It is cheaper to have it done by a local farmer or contractor.

The course builder should be on the site to supervise the earthmoving equipment. This not only prevents costly mistakes being made, but it is also a great opportunity to get value for money. When the water jump is excavated, the fill can be used to rough out a bank complex; ditches can be dug and gaps in fence-lines cleared. Heavy equipment operators generally enjoy the change of pace and are generous with advice on drainage and water management. All the planning decisions should be made before the earthmoving equipment arrives. Digging test holes for the potential water jump is part of the decision-making process. This can be done with a post-hole auger.

Cross-country courses devour a substantial amount of timber and the faint-hearted can have second thoughts when they see the materials list. No problem

– everything is available at a fraction of the cost if you know where to look. Sources can include: demolition yards, sawmills (ask for timber with defects), electrical contractors who install power poles (ask for the old and the damaged), golf courses and housing developments (both show little restraint when logging). It is important to have variety on a course and this is an opportunity for saving. Pine and poplar are cheap and, although they will rot in a few years, can provide the timber for lower level jumps that are quick to build. It makes sense to take advantage of what is cheap and available, so long as the jumps are easy to replace.

Creative course design is the easiest way to save money. There are drawbacks to multiple-use jumps, but they do enable you to have a quality course on a limited budget. The four main creative ways to build a course are:

**Reversible jumps.** Located on a slight incline, the lower level rides the fence in a downhill direction and the higher level rides it uphill.

**Adjustable height**. These are constructed so that the height can easily be altered.

**Combinations**. Different levels sharing part of the same combination.

**Knowledge**. The higher the level of experience, the greater the ideas for saving.

Brush jumps require a vast amount of brush. Some types of brush are far more attractive than others. Cedar, juniper and birch are the first choice, but any sapling, like willow or alder, can do the job. Competitions with a generous budget have the luxury of replacing the brush each year. I consider this a terrible waste. Vigorous pruning will take care of sharp spikes and by greening up the front and back, the jump will look like new.

Many courses would not be built on time or up to standard without the help of volunteers. The best are machete-wielding weekend warriors. Their lust for action has rendered them, like Viking berserkers, oblivious to heat or cold. For them, pain is just weakness leaving the body. Then there is the other kind, and for the course builder who has to supervise them, they are a nightmare. They roam onto the course with their station wagons loaded to the gunwales with food but bereft of tools. More accustomed to sedentary suburban life this is an alien environment for them. Hernias, hornets, ticks, mosquitoes, and poison ivy can all cause work stoppages. Someone once said that there are no extra bits in the universe, everything has a purpose. Volunteers are, no doubt, part of the big scheme of things, but they can be a mixed blessing.

# 4.

# Fences That Don't Work

At first glance, safety and galloping over fences might seem contradictory. Not necessarily so: hospital waiting rooms are filled with the unbooted public who choose not to view the world from between the tips of skis, the bow of a kayak or the ears of a horse. The reason why the thrill is real and the risks perceived is because course builders and officials understand the deceptions of design. A ditch and brush looks huge when viewed from the side, but to a galloping horse its shape is perfect for a bold leap. On the other hand, there are types of fence, construction and terrain that just don't mix. The three main concerns are construction, siting of jumps and unintentional illusions. In addition, there are two overarching factors that need to be considered – what is right and what is wrong changes with the levels of competition, and the need to appreciate the difference between the shabby and the shoddy.

Some courses can only be described as shabby. They are built on a shoestring that long ago became untied. These rhinestones in the rough deserve sympathetic support. They are built and run largely by volunteers and parents, who believe that enthusiasm alone will transport them across a trackless void of inexperience. Without their efforts many fine local courses would not exist. Then there are the shoddy. Whether it is because of spade-shy organisers or tame officials, these courses need to reevaluate their objectives.

It is useful to visualise a **safety zone**, for horse and rider, around each fence. This should extend at least 30ft (9m) in all directions. Low branches, exposed

CHAPTER 4 | **FENCES THAT DON'T WORK**

stumps and rocks are all potential hazards. Trees on the landing side of jumps can often be saved through creative design. A sudden change in footing in front of a fence can cause problems. If screenings or gravel are necessary for good footing then they should extend at least two strides in front of the jump. Sprinkling the screenings with grass clippings and a thin layer of topsoil will help blend it in with the surrounding area.

Poor construction is the easiest to recognise and change. The hallmarks of a good fence are a well-defined top- and ground-line, a solid appearance and an ascending profile. Horses have to be able to make the distinction between the 4in (10cm) diameter rails used in show jumping that will knock down and the solid, fixed fences on the cross-country course. This is achieved by using timber that is at least 8in (20cm) in diameter. Airy 2in x 6in (5cm x 15cm) construction, as once seen in picnic table and hay rack fences, with their sharp edges and false ground-lines, combine all the worst characteristics of a fence. Milled lumber certainly has its place on a course, but the finished product must look as though it belongs on a cross-country course.

Any fence that a horse could get caught up in has to be constructed so that it can be quickly dismantled and then speedily reassembled with no change in appearance. Rails are attached to posts with rope, and the sub-structure is held together with wire. Judicious use of a knife and wire-cutters can quickly dismantle the whole structure. It is worth taking a close look at some of the most popular fences.

**Table fences** have attracted some controversy, and no wonder; they are a diverse species. The worst look like unsympathetic packing crates with flags tacked on. The best will have a solid ascending front. The top will also be ascending, with at least a 2in (5cm) difference in height between the front and

Good and bad oxers.

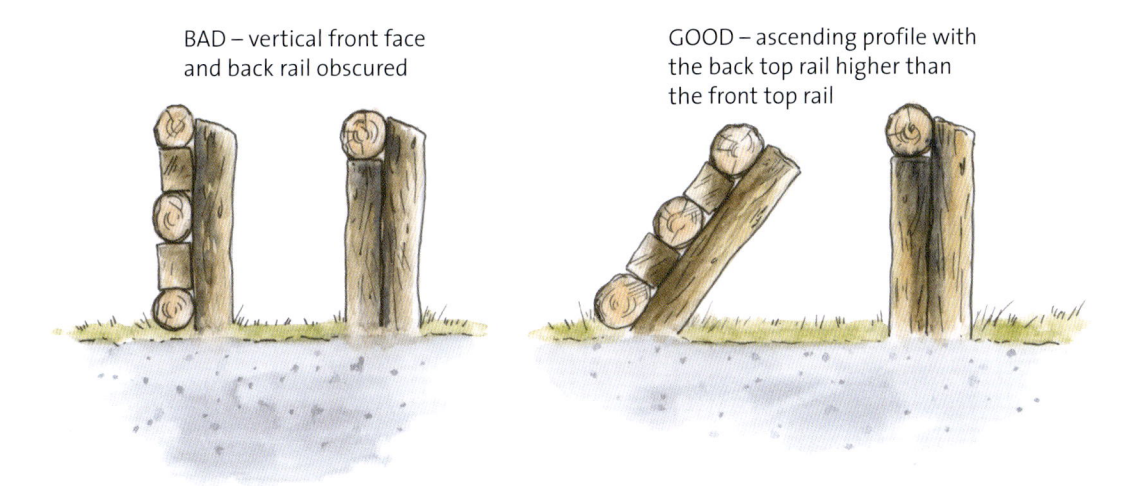

BAD – vertical front face and back rail obscured

GOOD – ascending profile with the back top rail higher than the front top rail

# DESIGN AND BUILD A **CROSS-COUNTRY COURSE**

the back. The top planks should be countersunk into the frame to give a smooth round edge. it is essential that size and spread of the fence is obvious to a galloping horse, and this is done by having an ascending profile and the front face either a solid ramp or built with at least 10in (25cm) diameter timber.

**Brush fences** are a great jump; they look big and ride well. Forgiving as they are to horses, they are unforgiving to builders. Packing the brush demands perseverance and dedication and is not a job to delegate to low-voltage personnel. The brush must be tightly packed so that there is no chance of a horse dropping a leg between the frame. Neatly trimmed, rather than wild and bushy, will encourage clean jumping. Sharp spikes will be exposed after the top is trimmed; these have to be cut right back and replaced with smaller sprigs of brush. Brush fences are jumped in stride and a good apron makes this possible. The apron is the lower front part of the jump and it should be solid enough to withstand a horse dropping a leg on it. One method to achieve this is to use tightly packed straw bales covered with taut woven synthetic fabric. Green brush is then woven into the fabric and this gives it a natural appearance.

**Vertical fences** seldom ride well. In certain situations, such as, after a turn, steep up hill or as the second element of a combination when a horse is naturally collected and jumping in stride, the risks are reduced. The argument for this type of fence is that it asks riders to jump correctly, rather than just fling themselves at a fence knowing that the apron will cover their mistakes. A better way to ask this question is using a pair of ascending rails, one stride apart and offset at close to 90°. If these are flagged as separate obstacles, then time and a run-out are the likely penalties rather than a fall. As a rule of thumb, all fences at the lower levels of competition should have an ascending profile and a positive ground-line.

The angle of the fence and the terrain determine the difficulty.

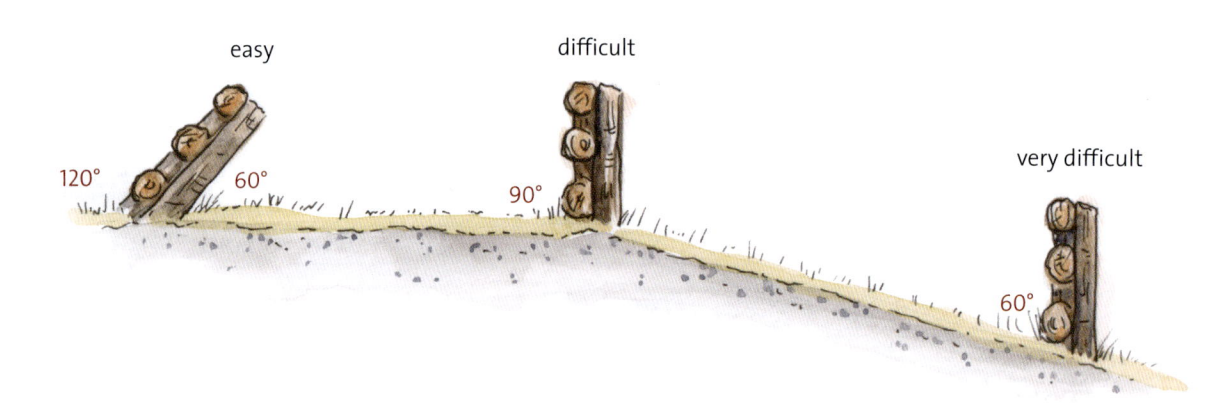

CHAPTER 4 | **FENCES THAT DON'T WORK**

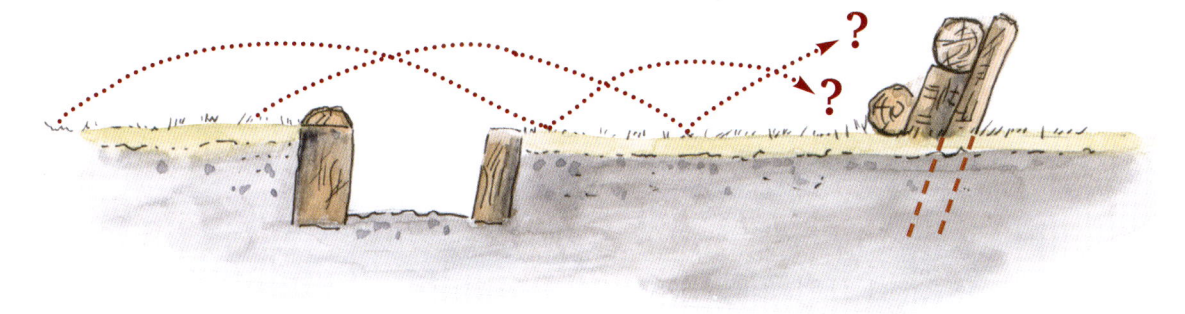

Striding problems can occur when a ditch is the first element of a combination.

The recent 'black flag' rule (see Glossary) has addressed a potential problem with **arrowhead** and **corner jumps**. This type of fence is a good test of accuracy and obedience. But if a horse swerves at the last moment and jumps to the side, it could get caught up in the protruding lower rail that forms the side element of the fence. Enlightened rule changes now recommend that there are three or more strides between option fences.

**Ditches** test training and experience rather than athletic ability, and they are an integral part of most courses. There is, however, one situation where they can unwittingly cause grief. A horse can clear a ditch regardless of whether it takes off 1ft (0.3m) or 6ft (1.8m) in front of the ditch. This can cause the next element to be off-stride. Consequently ditches belong as the middle element of a combination, when the horse is locked into a stride, rather than the first element.

**Water jumps** are often the most influential fences on the course. It should be remembered that spectators are horse people too, and flock to the

The footing in water jumps must stand up to a full competition of horses.

landing on level ground after a drop fence is hard on horses' legs and more likely to cause a hole to form in the landing area

sharp gravel increases risk of injury

25

sharp, rough bark

Logs should have a smooth surface.

sharp edges

Jumps must not have sharp edges.

challenging fences to watch displays of horsemanship and not horses and riders getting in trouble. The questions asked by the designer need to be carefully thought out. There are several factors to remember. A big spread fence into water asks a contradictory question. The spread fence calls for a big effort, but entry into water should be controlled and balanced to offset the drag effect of water. The depth of water should only be 6–9in (15–22cm), but you are working with nature and water levels can change quickly. It is better to have a modest fence into water and a more technical one exiting the water. This rewards riders who can keep riding with balance and accuracy through the combination. When there is a fence immediately after the water, the footing between the water and the jump should be gravel and not grass. A considerable amount of water runs off horses' legs when leaving the water. A full competition of horses can turn a grassy slope into a mudslide. The depth of water, the nature and the firmness of the footing all affect safety and must be thoroughly scrutinised.

A **maximum spread fence** with a big drop is not a good idea. Horses tend to put down their undercarriage too soon and can get caught up in the fence. A better choice in this situation is a solid ascending vertical. The fence should not be sited on the edge of a steep drop, but rather set back far enough so that the horse can land before the ground drops off steeply. Fences on a down slope must have a definite ascending profile. This reduces the chance of a horse taking off too late.

Horses repeatedly save their riders and will compensate for poor course design. Bad fences that ride successfully most of the time pose a real dilemma.

A full competition of horses may clear the fence, but past experience reinforces the nagging doubt that this is a problem fence. Top of the list of rogues is the maximum spread fence, particularly parallel rails after a long downhill gallop. Horses will be too much on the forehand when galloping downhill, but the rider will need to keep the horse well between hand and leg, without losing impulsion, to jump the fence. Experienced riders can manage this. But the reality is that no matter how strong you are, being able to hold a runaway horse downhill is just wishful thinking. In this situation the course should be redesigned so that after a long downhill gallop there is a turn before the next fence.

**Combinations on a down slope** should be viewed with caution. There is a place for them at the upper levels of competition, but the striding becomes unpredictable with the slope and the varying speed of competitors. Solid ramped fences or brush, rather than open rails, make good sense in this situation.

**Illusions**, intentional and unintentional, are the difference between a great course and a disaster. Equestrian sport is based on trust. The horse trusts the rider that he will not be asked to perform beyond his capabilities. The rider trusts the course builder that the fences are appropriate. Nevertheless, the designer's mandate is to create a competition, and riders are expected to rise to the challenge. This can be done successfully without a break in trust by using intentional illusions that will give the rider, rather than the horse, the collywobbles. There are numerous examples of how this is done. A big ditch and brush or trakehner can be intimidating when walking the course, but it is the horse that does the actual jumping and what really matters is what the galloping horse sees. Riders walking the course would do better if they paid less attention to the fence and more to the number one question – 'How should I present the horse to this fence?' Unintentional illusions need to be recognised before the competition begins. Many factors can affect a horse's vision. Shadows, a low sun late in the afternoon, a sudden change from light to dark can all play havoc with a perfectly innocuous fence.

Designers like to level the playing field. One way of doing this is by having a relatively small and straightforward fence on a turn just before a water jump. Little Susie will ride it beautifully because she will follow her coach's detailed instructions. But the professional may come whipping around the corner, fail to present the horse properly to the fence on account of it being so easy. The horse's attention, meanwhile, will be on the water complex and not on the fence, and he may duck out at the last minute.

The hinges of sport are held with little screws, to paraphrase Bismarck. Today, more than ever, there are conflicting elements that the designer has to balance. Courses are expected to be more technical, yet riders and horses have less background experience of riding cross-country. Safety concerns have increased the cost and complexities for organisers and course builders. It is debatable how much the course should do the riding for the riders in the quest for safer courses. If there is an answer, I believe that it is in understanding the subtleties of intentional and unintentional illusions.

# 5.

# Footing

Course builders have to be footing specialists. This means recognising all the potential problems and having the right answers. It is the footing or track surface that poses the real risk to horses and expense to horse people. Competitors are well aware of this and, like drivers avoiding bad roads, they will shun a competition with a reputation for bad footing.

A basic understanding of the biomechanics of galloping helps us to grasp what is required for optimum footing. A horse's legs act as a spring; the ground also acts as a spring, pushing back against the impact of each hoof as it hits the ground. Under ideal conditions, such as old turf, both forces act in unison, creating effortless galloping. If the ground is too hard or too soft the track will feel dead, and stress damage will begin sooner rather than later.

Horses' legs depend upon the love life of the earthworm. This is only a slight exaggeration. The ideal riding surface is well-established turf. It has cushion, is resilient to damage and drains well. Earthworms are responsible for making and maintaining good turf. They like to come to the surface at night to breed and feed on organic matter. Worms work their way to the surface by eating dirt. This mixes with calcium carbonate in their stomach and passes through as mineral-rich castings.

The holes they make allow air and water to penetrate the different layers of soil, and this has earned them the reputation as nature's ploughmen. Generously manuring the course in the autumn will keep both horses and worms happy.

Manure and mowing are the long-term answers to improving the track. It is, however, the various grades and types of gravel that are used which ensure immediate good footing. The coarser grades are used beneath the surface to strengthen the ground and promote good drainage, while the finer grades, like screenings, provide a safe, firm jumping surface.

Gravel has two origins: pit-run or crusher-run (see Glossary for definition of gravel terms). Pit-run is rounded and comes from river or glacial out-wash deposits. Because it is rounded, it is not so easy to pack and, depending on where you live, can be more readily available and cheaper. The cost is in the trucking. Ungraded pit-run is a natural mix of stones, sand and gravel and is generally the cheapest material for backfilling behind revetting or retaining walls and as the base layer for roads. A good all-purpose gravel for cross-country is 0–¾ in (20mm) graded pit-run. Crusher-run refers to rocks that have been passed through a mill. The 5–6in (12.5–15cm) diameter grade is called rip-rap. It is the best material for a base layer, but can be expensive. The 0–¾ in (20mm) crusher-run is sharp and angular; consequently it packs and binds well. Because it is sharp a top dressing of screenings or topsoil will generally be necessary. The finest grades of crusher-run are called crusher dust, screenings or scalpings. It makes an excellent riding surface, so long as it is packed to the right density. Without packing it is soft and shifting, but if packed too much it will become rock hard. Driving on it with a tractor, so long as the crusher dust is damp, will result in the correct firmness. It can then be ridden on right away. The following year if it is too firm, add a thin layer of topsoil to encourage grass to grow and provide cushion. Adding screenings to soft or sandy ground is generally counterproductive. In this scenario a geotextile fabric is used to keep the sub-surface and the footing separate.

Geotextile membrane is the generic term for the synthetic fabric that is widely used commercially to keep gravel separate from the subsoil, whether it is in building highways or septic systems. It represents a considerable saving in gravel and heavy equipment time. If there is a magic bullet to guaranteeing immediate and long-term good footing, this is it. Understanding the concept is more important than using exactly the right fabric for the job. Old tarpaulins or other woven synthetic fabrics will do the job, as they only have to last long enough for the gravel to set. The gravel will then become the barrier. Old household carpets have been used, but because of chemicals leaching out of them and into the soil, they are considered environmentally toxic. The geotextile membrane is installed by thoroughly covering the area with at least one layer of the fabric and then carefully covering that with 6in (15cm) of gravel. When spreading the gravel, be careful to drive on it and not the fabric, or you will want to throw this book and everything else into the morass and walk away. The gravel will pack down to 4in (10cm) and can generally be ridden on immediately, but it is better to give it a few months to set.

The footing on either side of a fence is critical. It must stay sound and consistent throughout the competition, regardless of the number of horses or the weather. The best way to ensure this is to have a layer of gravel just beneath the surface. This should be done when the fence is being built. Remove the topsoil, lay down 4in (10cm) of gravel, and then replace the topsoil and seed. Tearing up the turf in front of a fence is a decision not to be taken lightly, but for the upper levels of competition or any fence on low-lying ground, it is worth the expense.

It is essential to prevent erosion and loss of topsoil whenever land is cleared and the soil is exposed to the elements. If the conditions are not right for germination, a covering of manure or old hay will prevent erosion under normal conditions. If small gullies start to form, block them with bales of straw before the damage escalates. To green up a site quickly, sow a mix of grass seed and a cereal, such as barley or wheat. The cereal can be up in ten days. This provides protection for the slower germinating grass seed. Grass does not grow by luck. It must be nurtured. Prepare the seed bed with thorough raking. Broadcast the seed, then carefully rake the seed into the topsoil. Covering it with a light mulch of old hay or manure will give it optimum conditions for germination and protection from wind and rain. Grass seed passes through a horse's digestive system intact and a cheaper alternative to seeding is to spread a thick layer of manure. However, weeds will come up first, as they are more aggressive colonisers than grasses.

There is a tendency to mow the track far too short. This may give the course all the neatness of a suburban lawn, but it is not good for horses or footing. The experts on turf are the racecourse clerks of the course. On flat-race courses, 4–6in (10–15cm) of grass is recommended and considered optimal for the generally lighter-framed flat-race horse. On steeplechase courses, 6–9in (15–23cm) is recommended. To repair the damage after a race meet, the divots are tamped back and clean brick sand is used to fill any remaining holes. If too much sand is used there is a tendency for the ground to get too firm in dry weather. Mechanical aerators will improve the cushion when the ground becomes too hard. There are several different designs and types, but they all aerate the soil, break it up and encourage root growth. Aerators must be used intelligently. A thunderstorm can turn the ground into a quagmire as the holes they make fill up with water, rather than have the rain quickly running off the surface. Adding material on the landing side of jumps does provide cushion and takes the sting out of the ground, but this is a difficult judgement call. The risk is that it will make the footing slippery. Peat moss is generally considered the best material for this job.

Leaf-mould and damp conditions make the footing in woodland slippery and unreliable. Clearing out the undergrowth and limbing trees on either side of the track helps to let the sunlight in and the grass to grow. Tracks through woodland should have a dressing of gravel or screenings. A top dressing of shavings manure will provide the cushion. Straw manure is too slippery to use until it is well rotted. Introducing the red wriggler earthworm or its cousin, the European Night Crawler, to your manure pile can turn it into friable compost relatively quickly. Red wrigglers are the doyens of the composting world and are widely available. They eat their own weight of material every day. The breeding stock has to be placed at the outside of the manure pile or the heat will kill them. This compost can then be used for cushion on hard or rough ground or to give life to soil poor in organic matter.

Exposed roots, spikes from mown shrubs, holes from livestock and other animals, rocks and rough ground – these are all hazards that have to be rectified. There is no magic fix to clearing the track. It requires hard work and diligence. The time and cost of the course preparation have to be included in the schedule and budget. The major footing problems are generally taken care of when the course is being built. The seemingly minor jobs, such as, repairing the footing around jumps, is often left until the last minute. Allow at least two days for this work so that it is not compromised by lack of time, cash or workers. The job must be done right: for example, filling a hole with topsoil instead of rocks and gravel will result in a treacherous mud hole after heavy rain.

There are pros and cons as to what type of gravel works best to repair the footing at fences. A dressing of screenings works well if it is less than 4in (10cm) deep, but it does smother the grass. It should be spread back two strides in front of the fence and dressed with a sprinkling of grass and topsoil. A sudden change in the appearance of the ground in front of a fence is an unnecessary distraction. Deeply cut-up ground requires a base of coarser gravel and a top dressing of screenings. An alternative to screenings is pit-run 0-3/4" gravel. This will pack well and grass will eventually grow through it. The more jumps are used, the better the footing. This is achieved by raking and adding a small amount of gravel as required. The gravel blends with the topsoil and creates perfect all-weather footing. It is easy to repair the footing at a fence, but not the complete track. This would be a reason for not allowing the course to be used in wet conditions. Replacing divots and rolling the course is expensive.

The first choice for wet or waterlogged areas is to stay away from them. If that is not an option, no problem – a sound galloping track can be made through a swamp if necessary. The first step is to consider drainage. But drainage only works if there is a fall in the ground allowing the water to flow away. After doing whatever drainage is feasible, a raised roadway is built over the wet ground. This is where geotextile membrane really comes into its own and represents a significant saving in material and labour. If the ground is really soft, a corduroy road will first have to be built. To do this, lay down a bed of logs across the track and cover these with one or more layers of the membrane. Carefully cover the fabric with 6in (15cm) of gravel. If you have taken short cuts, it will become apparent when you pack it with the tractor. (See Chapter 12.) If it is well packed, the track can be used right away, but the real benefit is apparent the following year, by which time it will be a firm roadway and too hard for galloping on. Add a top dressing of shavings manure to provide a cushion and to get some grass established. Shavings manure or other compost can be very effective in providing a good cushion on hard rough ground, such as a gravel track. However, it can become treacherously slippery in wet weather.

# 6.

# Striding

There is no rosetta stone of striding. That does not mean that knowing the right distance between elements in a combination is a challenge. It's not, at least not on level ground. However, it takes considerable skill to decipher all the variables that can affect a horse's stride. The fences, like the Pyramids, grab the spotlight, but it is the interpretation of the empty space between the jumps that reveals the secret of how the combination will ride. Getting the striding right is one of the most important ways that a course designer can influence the safety of a course and keep the risks more perceived than real. Learning how to get the distances right between elements of a combination is fortunately not difficult. On level ground the measurements are uncomplicated. Sloping ground is more difficult to assess because a horse's stride generally lengthens on gentle downhill slopes, but shortens considerably on steeper uphill or downhill grades.

The course builder has to be an authority on striding and can use this knowledge to influence how a combination will ride. For example, marginally shorter striding asks for more control and less speed, and this gives the horse more time to see what is expected of him. But if the striding is on the short side you can expect to see unpleasant riding from competitors on longer-striding horses. The designer has to decide the optimum distance for the average horse ridden at the right pace, and has to trust the competitors to make any minor adjustments that are necessary for their horse.

Every combination is affected by a different set of variables and working these all out is one of the defining roles of a course designer. There are three ways to measure the distance between elements of a combination:

1. Simply take a tape measure and determine the distance between the back of the first element and the front of the second one.

2. Know the distance of your own stride and walk out the distance between the two fences. Learning to walk with a three-foot stride makes this a quick and convenient way to assess distances.

3. Judge where the average horse will land and, starting at this point, count out the number of your strides to the point of take-off for the second element. This assumes that four of your strides will equal one 12ft (3.6m) horse stride.

It is critical to get it right the first time and it is worth following the advice of the carpenter's adage – 'measure twice, cut once'. The table of distances is given in the spirit of putting builders on the right track. The final decision must be made by the person on the ground.

### STANDARD DISTANCES FOR FENCES ON LEVEL GROUND

| | |
|---|---|
| Bounce | 13ft–15ft (3.9m–4.5m) |
| 1 stride | 24ft–25ft (7.2m–7.5m) |
| 2 strides | 35ft–36ft (10.5m–10.8m) |
| Rails to ditch or ditch to rails | 20ft–21ft (6m–6.3m) |
| Rails to water or water to rails | 20ft–21ft (6m–6.3m) |
| Step (bounce) | 9ft–10ft (2.7m–3m) |
| Step (one stride) | 17ft 6in–20ft (5.25m–6m) |
| Normandy bank (bounce) | 10ft 6in–11ft 6in (3.15m–3.45m) |
| Normandy bank (one stride) | 17ft 6in–19ft 6in (5.25m–5.85m) |

- For fences with more than two strides, add 12ft (3.6m) per stride.
- The striding in water jumps and on banks is generally measured in 10ft (3m) increments.

## Variables affecting striding

- A horse's stride is longer on a gentle downhill slope, but shortens considerably on steeper grades.

- If the striding between fences is on the long side this results in riders being too aggressive and the extra speed gives the horse less time to assess the obstacle. Conversely, when the distance is short not only is there a risk of hitting the second element, but also unnecessary rating (taking a pull or a series of aggressive half-halts) on the approach upsets the horse and destroys rhythm and balance.

- The striding in combinations with either ditches or steps is 3ft (0.9m) less than it would be with regular fences with height, such as rails or tables. For example, rails to a ditch is 21ft (6.3m) rather than 24ft (7.2m).

- The shorter distances on banks and steps is because horses get their undercarriage down quicker as the landing is 3ft (0.9m) higher than the take-off.

- Ditches can be jumped successfully regardless of whether the horse takes off from 1ft (30cm) or 5ft (1.5m) in front of the ditch. However, this can throw off the striding to the next element. Consequently coffin combinations are rails-to-ditch-to-rails. The first element sets up the striding so that it becomes a straightforward gymnastic exercise. Ditches do serve a useful role in helping horses to take off at the optimum point. For example, a small ditch in front of a bounce Normandy bank helps a horse land and take off from the right spot on the bank.

- The distance for the striding is measured from the back of the first element to the front of the second element. The exception is a bounce fence; this is measured from the centre of both the elements.

- It is important to note that striding distances are not written in stone and experience and good judgement have to be used to evaluate each situation individually.

# 7.

# Portable Fences

Portable fences are indispensable to building cost-effective and versatile courses. They enable the designer to change the route and the level of difficulty at minimal cost. Furthermore, they can be built indoors during the off-season. It is important to keep in mind when building these types of jumps that they should be structurally robust and look as though they belong on a cross-country course. Portables are a boon if used with discretion and restraint. However, they are the 'fast food' of course building, and riders and horses deserve better than to be served up the jumping equivalent of hamburgers, no matter how well dressed.

There are many styles and designs of portable jumps. The five described here are easy to build and can be adapted for every level of competition. I can't overstate how necessary it is to use your judgement as well as the rule book when deciding on the dimensions when building these jumps. Professional builders recognise that every jump is a proposal, albeit a strong proposal, that has to be accepted by, at the very least, the technical delegate and ground jury. Many a time have I had to lower portable fences, either with a chainsaw or spade, because the organiser/builder failed to read the words 'maximum' and 'appropriate' in the rule book. As a rule of thumb it is better to build them at least 3in (75mm) lower than you think they should be. It is much easier to jack them up with a plank than to dig them in, or worse, have your beloved chainsaw ripping into nails. Rule books also require that all portables be securely staked. This can be done either with half-round wooden stakes or steel rods that have holes so that they can be fastened to the jump. The stakes are more effective if positioned closer to the front rather than the back of the fence; obviously the most important criterion is that they work and don't pose an additional hazard.

## Portable ascending rails

This fence consists of a pair of equilateral triangular frames that support ascending rails. The height of the rails can be adjusted easily without tools or equipment. This makes them particularly useful for training centres. However, moving them can be tricky without taking the rails off the frames. The frame is made by sandwiching a pair of short posts between two half-rounds to form an equilateral triangle. The rails are roped to the sloping sides of the frames, which stand 4ft 6in (1.35m) high.

### MATERIALS

- 3 rails approx. 14ft–16ft (4.2m–4.8m) long and approx. 10in (25cm) diameter (rails)
- 4 posts @ 4ft 6in (1.35m) and 8in (20cm) diameter (end frames)
- 2 logs @ 5ft (1.5m) and 10in (25cm) diameter (to be ripped for bases of frames)
- 1 post @ 4ft (1.2m) and 8in (20cm) diameter (blocks)
- 18 nails @ 8in (20cm) long
- 10ft (3m) of ⅜in (10mm) nylon rope
- 6ft (1.8m) of mild steel wire and handful of 1½in (35mm) staples
- 2 x 3ft (90cm) long and 6in (15cm) diameter half-rounds (stakes)

### CONSTRUCTION METHOD

- Take two 4ft 6in (1.35m) posts. Lay them on the ground in the shape of a vee. One of the posts should extend 9in (23cm) past the other.
- Rip a 10in (25cm) diameter 5ft (1.5m) long log into a pair of half-rounds. These will become the base.

CHAPTER 7 | **PORTABLE FENCES**

Portable ascending rails.

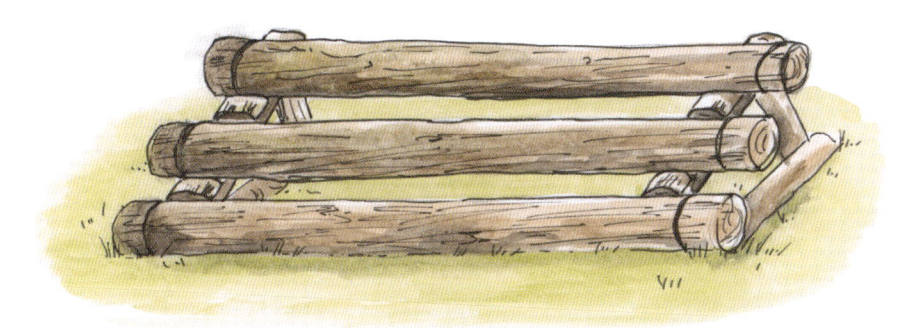

- Place one half-round across the lower end of the posts so that it forms the third side of the triangle.

- Adjust the sides to form an equilateral triangle with a 4ft 6in (1.35m) base. Trim the top join to ensure a tight fit. Check the measurements and adjust as necessary.

- Nail the top join together, and then nail the half-round to the lower end of the posts.

- Turn the frame over and nail on the other half-round. Trim off the ends of the half-rounds.

- Build a second frame using the same measurements as the first.

- Wire the largest of the three rails to the base of the frames. Short blocks separate the other two rails. The weight of the rails holds the blocks in place. The height of the fence is adjusted by altering the size of the blocks.

- Rope the two rails to the frames. The fence will now be rigid. Stake as required.

- The fence can be ridden from both directions if a 12in (30cm) diameter log is placed on the inside of the frames. If this is planned, then it is better to use two 10in (25cm) rails rather than three 8in (20cm) ones. This keeps the rails in proportion and avoids the possibility of the fence having a false ground-line. The centre can be packed with brush if it needs to be made very inviting.

Alternative style – can be ridden from either direction.

39

## Portable roll top

Roll tops are among the most versatile of all jumps. They can be jumped from either direction, are easy to move and fit well with existing fences when used to form combinations. The width of the base combined with their weight makes them very stable. A roll top is made from a pair of frames onto which are nailed half-rounds. The finished jump looks like a roll of logs. The dimensions of the frames will depend upon the level of competition that they are going to be used for. The top of the frame should be at least 6in (15cm) lower than the maximum top height of the finished jump. Using half-rounds ripped from logs of 9in–12in (23cm–30cm) diameter ensures that the fence is solid and looks like a cross-country jump. An internal subframe may be necessary if planks are used instead of half-rounds.

### MATERIALS

> Approx. 6 logs @ 12ft (3.6m) with a minimum diameter of 10in (25cm) (ripped into half-rounds)
>
> 2 posts @ 5ft (1.5m) long and a minimum diameter of 8in (20cm) (ripped into half-rounds)
>
> 2 posts @ 2ft (60cm) long and 8in (20cm) diameter (ripped into half-rounds)
>
> 4 posts @ 4ft (1.2m) long and 8in (20cm) diameter (frame)
>
> 2 x 3ft (90cm) long and 6in (15cm) diameter half-rounds (stakes)
>
> 10lbs (5kg) of 8in (20cm) nails

### CONSTRUCTION METHOD

- Lay two 4ft (1.2m) posts on the ground so that they form a vee.

- Place a 5ft (1.5m) half-round on the posts so that it forms the base of the triangle. Then take the 2ft (60cm) half-round and place it on the posts just below the point where they join. Adjust the posts and the half-rounds so that it is a quadrangle with the base approximately four times longer than the top. The height of the frame should be at least 6in (15cm) lower than the height of the finished jump.

CHAPTER 7 | **PORTABLE FENCES**

Portable roll top. *(Photo: Claus Zander)*

the protruding ends of posts and half-rounds are trimmed off

60°

60° angle is important for stability and ridability

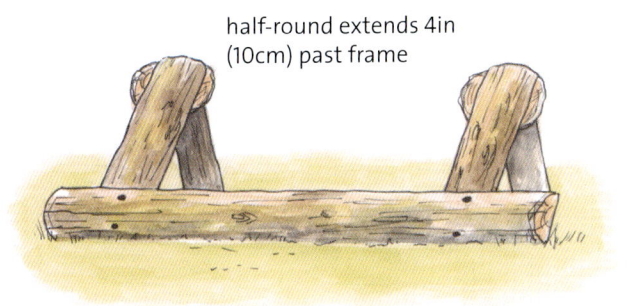

half-round extends 4in (10cm) past frame

roll top with max outside dimensions, just under 3ft (90cm) high and 4ft (1.2m) base spread

41

- Nail the half-rounds to the posts. Then turn the frame over and nail the other two half-rounds onto the posts. The posts will now be sandwiched between a 5ft (1.5m) and a 2ft (60cm) pair of half-rounds. Trim off the protruding ends of the posts and the half-rounds.

- Rip at least five or six logs into half-rounds. The logs should be not less than 12ft (3.6m) long and 10in (25cm) in diameter.

- Stand the frames upright and 11ft (3.3m) apart (if using 12ft/3.6m half-rounds). Place the half-rounds against the frames and trim and fit as necessary. Nail the half-rounds to the frames.

## Portable flower box

The profile of this jump is similar to a roll top except that the top is wider and is countersunk. The 6in-deep recessed top will be filled with mulch or peat moss and decorated with flowers. It is an on-going challenge for course builders to make a splash without cash. These jumps provide colour without undue expense.

Portable flower box with countersunk top. *(Photo: Charlotte Harper)*

## MATERIALS

- 3 or 4 logs @ 12–14ft (3.6–4.2m) with a minimum diameter of 10in (25cm) (ripped into half-rounds)

- 4 posts @ 4ft (1.2m) long and 8in (20cm) diameter (uprights for frames)

- 1 log @ 5ft (1.5m) long and 9in (23cm) diameter (ripped to become base of the frame)

- 1 log @ 3ft (90cm) long and 9in (23cm) diameter (ripped to become top of the frame)

- 1 or 2 logs @ 4ft (1.2cm) long and 9in (23cm) diameter (ripped to fill outside of the frame)

- 6 pressure-treated planks, 2in x 6in (5cm x 15cm) and 12ft (3.6m) long (deck and support brace)

- 2 x 3ft (90cm) long and 6in (15cm) diameter half-rounds (stakes)

- 10lbs (5kg) of 8in (200mm) nails and 2lbs (1kg) of 4in (100mm) nails

- Flowers and mulch

## CONSTRUCTION METHOD

- Lay two 4ft (1.2m) posts on the ground. Angle them so that the tops are 2ft (60cm) apart and the bottoms are 4ft 6in (1.35m) apart.

- Place a 5ft (1.5m) half-round across the wide end of the posts and the 3ft (90cm) half-round across the other end. The dimensions of the frames will depend upon the level of competition that the jump is for. (The height of the frame should be at least 6in (15cm) below the maximum top height allowed for the competition it is being built for. Also, check the base width is within the rules.)

- Check the top and bottom spread and the height and adjust the half-rounds as necessary. A base 4ft 6in (1.35m) wide and a top 2ft (60cm) wide would be in proportion. Nail the half-rounds to the posts and trim off the protruding ends. Add one or more half-rounds between the ones already nailed so that there are no gaps.

- Rip three or four logs that are about 10in (25cm) in diameter and 12ft–14ft (3.6m–4.2m) long.

- Position the frames so that they are upright and just under 12ft (3.6m) apart (if that is the length of the half-round).

- Nail two or three half-rounds to each side of the frame. The top of the top half-round should be at least 6in (15cm) below the maximum height allowed for the level of competition.

- Build a sturdy deck on the inside of the frame. The deck is 6in (15cm) below the top of the jump. It is easiest to make the deck out of 2in x 6in (5cm x 15cm) pressure-treated planks. A centre support brace is necessary so that the planks can support a wayward horse.

- Fill the deck with mulch or peat moss and dress with flowers. A live ground-cover plant and bright synthetic flowers work well.

## Portable flower box with top rail

This is a similar jump to the flower box. The differences are that its sides are lower, the deck is flush with the top of the sides and it has a log suspended across the top. The advantages are that it looks good with or without decoration, and because it has a log, rather than a top spread, it is very inviting.

Portable flower box with top rail. *(Photo: Claus Zander)*

## MATERIALS

- 2 logs @ 12ft (3.6m) with a minimum diameter of 10in (25cm) (ripped into half-rounds)

- 4 posts @ 4ft (1.2m) long and 6in (15cm) diameter (uprights of frames)

- 1 log @ 14ft (4.20m) long and minimum 8in (20cm) diameter (top log)

- 2 logs @ 5ft (1.5m) long and 9in (23cm) diameter (ripped to become the base of the frame)

- 1 log @ 4ft (1.2m) long and 9in (23cm) diameter (ripped to become the top of the frame)

- 6 pressure-treated planks, 2in x 6in (5cm x 15cm) and 12ft (3.6m) long (deck)

- 2 x 3ft (90cm) long and 6in (15cm) diameter half-rounds (stakes)

- 8lbs (4kg) of 8in (200mm) nails

- 2lbs (1kg) of 4in (100mm) nails

## CONSTRUCTION METHOD

- Lay the two 4ft (1.2m) posts on the ground. Angle them so that the bottoms are 3ft 6in (1.05m) apart and the tops join to form a vee.

- Place a 4ft (1.2m) half-round across the wide end of the posts and a 2ft 6in (75cm) half-round 12in (30cm) below the tops of the posts.

- Follow the directions for building a flower box (page 42), except that the sides are only two half-rounds high (approx. 1ft 9in–2ft/52.5cm–60cm).

- Plank the deck. The planks should be parallel with the ends rather than the sides, i.e. they are nailed to the half-rounds rather than to the frame ends.

- Trim off the top of the posts so that they are 6in (15cm) higher than the top of the frame. The top log is slotted in between these posts. Both the log and the frame will need to be trimmed to ensure a snug fit. Rope the log to the uprights.

- A suggestion is to paint the deck black. Potted plants can be placed on the deck. However, it works well without decoration.

## Portable parallel rails or oxer

This is another versatile portable jump. It can easily be adapted to become a table or farm shelter. Another advantage is that the height and top spread are simple to adjust without tools or equipment – a bonus for training centres. The frames consist of a pair of thick, short posts; their base is sandwiched between half-rounds, and a post is notched so that it fits across the top of the vertical posts. The frame looks like an old-fashioned canon when looked at from the side. Three rails are required. The biggest one rests on the base of the frame and the other two are positioned across the top of the frame to become the parallel rails. The back of the frame is 3in (15cm) higher than the front. By sliding the top back rail onto the frame the height as well as the top spread are increased. The fence becomes rigid by roping the rails securely to the frame.

To turn the jump into a table, simply plank the two top rails together. The planks should be countersunk into the rails so that a rounded edge is presented to horses. This requires using 10in–12in (25cm–30cm) rails, so that there is no airy gap in the front face of the table.

To make a farm shelter the rails are ripped into half-rounds and these are nailed onto the front and top.

Portable parallel rails or oxer. *(Photo: Claus Zander)*

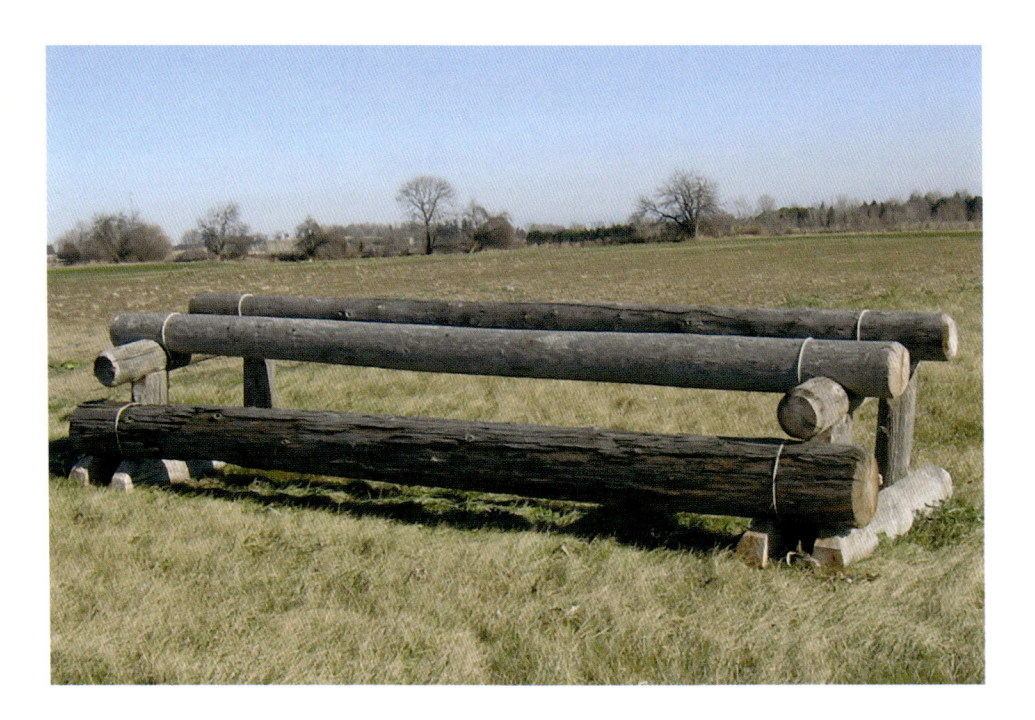

CHAPTER 7 | **PORTABLE FENCES**

## MATERIALS

- 2 logs @ 6ft (1.8m) long and 10in (25cm) diameter (ripped to become base of the frame)

- 2 logs @ 6ft (1.8m) long and 9in (23cm) diameter (top of the frame)

- 2 logs @ 2ft 6in (75cm) and 8in (20cm) diameter (front upright part of the frame)

- 2 logs @ 2ft 9in (82.5cm) and 8in (20cm) diameter (back upright part of the frame)

- 3 logs @ 16ft (4.8m) long and 10in (25cm) diameter (ground and top rails)

- 2 x 3ft (90cm) long and 6in (15cm) diameter half-rounds (stakes)

- 5lbs (2.5kg) of 8in (20cm) nails

- 20ft (6m) of ³⁄₈ in (10mm) nylon rope

## CONSTRUCTION METHOD

- Cut the timber for the frame. Two short posts – 2ft 6in (75cm) and 2ft 9in (82.5cm) long, two half-rounds 6ft (1.8m) long and 9in (23cm) in diameter.

- Lay the two short posts on the ground so that they are parallel and 4ft

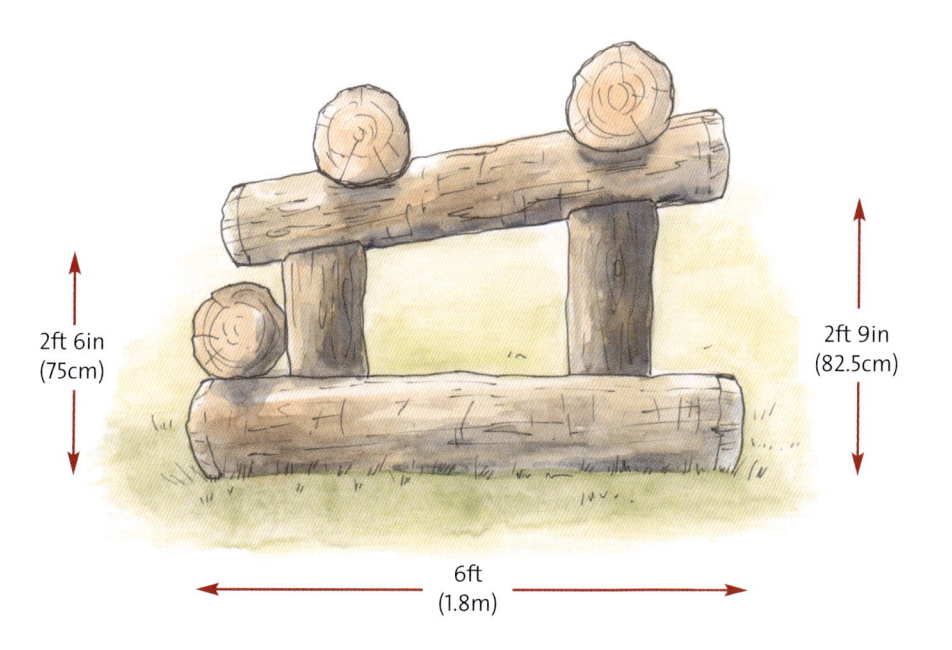

Side view of portable oxer.

2ft 6in (75cm)

2ft 9in (82.5cm)

6ft (1.8m)

47

# DESIGN AND BUILD A CROSS-COUNTRY COURSE

(1.2m) apart (outside to outside measurement).

- Nail a half-round to the base end of the posts. Check the measurements so that the half-round extends 1ft (30cm) on either side of the posts. Turn the frame over and nail the other half-round onto the posts so that the posts are evenly sandwiched between the half-rounds.

- Stand the frame upright and check that the posts are vertical. Square the top of the upright posts. Place the 6ft (1.8m) top log on top of the short posts. Use small wedges to keep it in place. Adjust the top log so that it extends 9in (23cm) on the landing side and 6in (15cm) on the take-off side.

- Notches will need to be cut out of the lower side of the top log. The tops of the posts fit into these notches. The notches are 2in (5cm) deep.

- Fit the top log onto the vertical posts. The joints will need to be trimmed to ensure a tight fit. When satisfied with the height and profile, nail the top log securely to the vertical posts.

- Build a second frame so that it is a duplicate of the first.

- The largest of the three rails is the ground-line. Position this on the half-rounds that extend to the front of the frames. It is tightly roped to the frame. The other two rails are positioned on the top log of the frame. The front top rail is positioned approximately over the front post. The back rail is placed toward the back of the frame. Cut a saddle notch into the rails so that they fit the top log of the frame. Rope the rails to the frame. The back rail will be about 3in (7.5cm) higher than the front one, and by sliding the back rail the spread and height can be adjusted.

## TIPS ON BUILDING PORTABLES

- These instructions and dimensions are for portables in the 3ft–3ft 6in (90–105cm) range. The trick to building the right size jump is to check the height and base spread dimensions, along with a critical look at the profile, when laying out the frame on the ground.

- The frames for these jumps are all made from short lengths of timber,

- which is often available at lower cost. Choose timber that will have at least a ten-year life.

- Double-nail the half-rounds with 8in (200mm) nails. Tractors are harder on portables than horses.

- See the tricks of the trade chapter (Chapter 12) for more advice on ripping logs.

- The five portables described here have a low centre of gravity and are heavy; this makes them very stable. Competition rules will require them to be staked. Custom-made stakes cut from steel rods are easy to drive into the ground and unobtrusive.

- Building portables using 8–12in (200–300mm) nails is quick and effective. Alternatives are discussed in Chapter 12.

# 8.

# Mainstay Fences

This chapter describes how to build fourteen of the most useful cross-country fences. The instructions can be adapted to build fences for any level of competition. However, there are even simpler methods for building lower-level jumps and these are described in Chapter 13, on Pony Club course building.

> **CAUTION**
>
> There are risks involved in any type of construction, and course building is no exception. The principal concerns are the safe operation of chainsaws and farm machinery. It is highly recommended and, in some cases, required by law, to take safety courses and follow safety procedures. This education should then be supplemented with an informal internship with professional designers and builders.

## Post and rails (two versions)

Ascending post and rail fences in various forms are the mainstay of cross-country courses. The construction technique used to build them is also the basis of many other types of jump. The gaps between the rails should be either small enough so that a horse cannot put a foot between them or large enough so that a leg can easily be lifted out between the rails. A clenched fist is a handy reference for the diameter of a gap that is cause for concern. There are two main construction techniques:

1. Vertical posts with the rails on support posts, which are either nailed or wired to the posts in the ground.

2. The posts are set at a 60° angle with the rails against the posts and separated by short blocks.

## MATERIALS

> 3 logs @ 16ft–18ft (4.8m–5.4m) long and approx 10in (25cm) diameter (rails)
>
> 3 posts @ 8ft (2.4m) long and 8in (20cm) diameter (posts and support blocks for rails)
>
> 10ft (3m) of nylon rope
>
> 6ft (1.8m) of mild steel wire and handful of 1½in (35mm) staples

## CONSTRUCTION METHOD (VERSION 1)

- Set a pair of posts in the ground. The holes should be at least 3ft (90cm) deep and approximately 16ft (4.8m) apart. Use the level to check that the post is vertical before you tamp.

- The proposed height of the top rail is marked on the posts with a lumber crayon. If a visual reference is necessary to help decide the height, then use a tight nylon line fastened to the posts to represent the top rail. This helps particularly when building on a slope, or for post and rails with a convex face.

- Place the rails on the ground. The thick and thin ends are alternated. When the jump is being built, the larger diameter rails will be closer to the ground. This helps to achieve the ascending profile.

- Measure the diameter of both ends of the top rail. Mark the posts so that you will know the height of the bottom of the rail. Measure from here to the

DESIGN AND BUILD A **CROSS-COUNTRY COURSE**

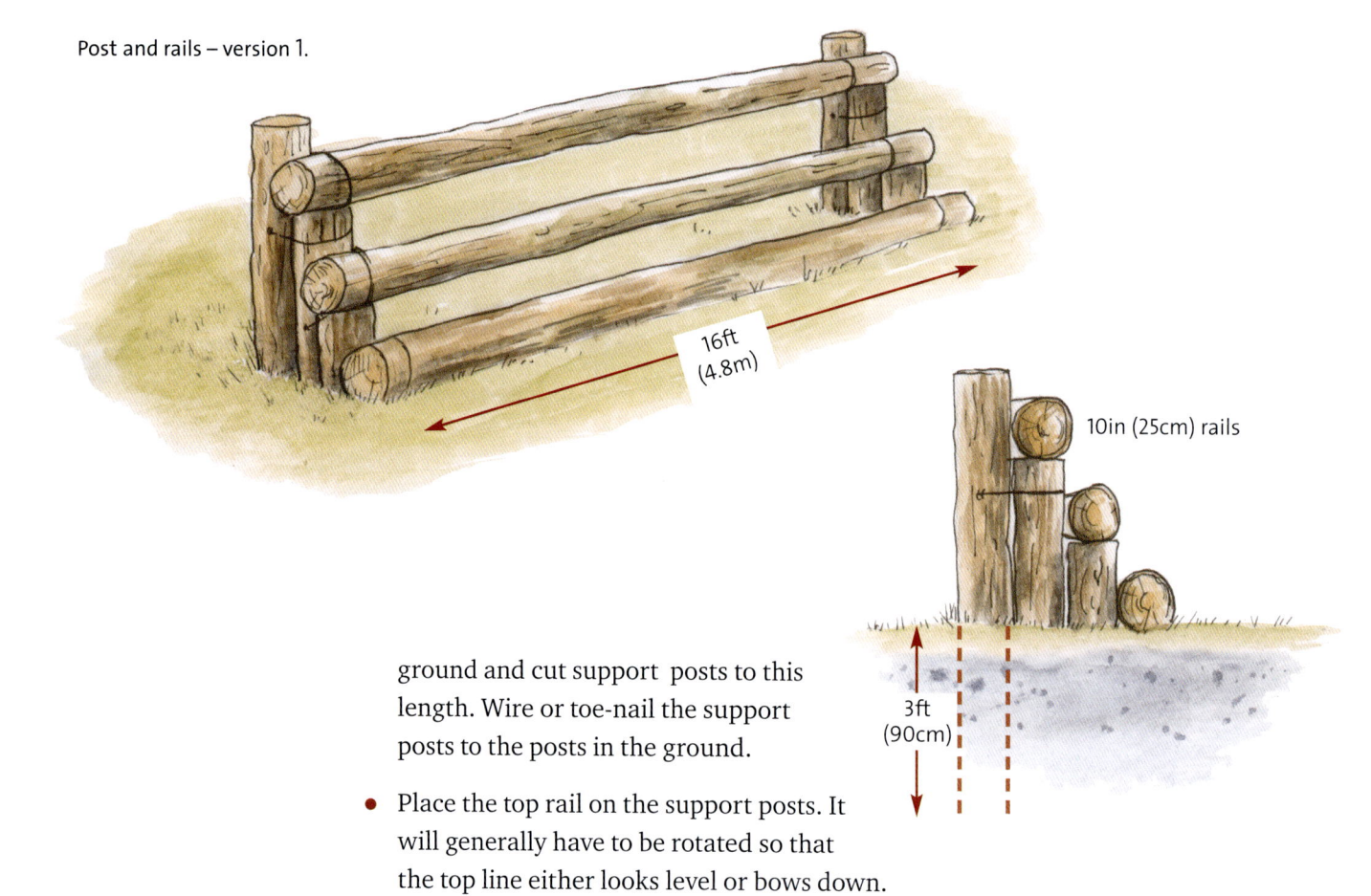

Post and rails – version 1.

16ft (4.8m)

10in (25cm) rails

3ft (90cm)

ground and cut support posts to this length. Wire or toe-nail the support posts to the posts in the ground.

- Place the top rail on the support posts. It will generally have to be rotated so that the top line either looks level or bows down.

- Two or three rails are used; this will depend on the height of the jump and the diameter of the rails. As a rule of thumb there should be more timber than gap. Repeat the procedure for the lower rails. To ensure that the fence looks balanced, the lower, middle and top rail should be an equal distance apart, the thick and thin ends of the rails being alternated.

- Measure the height of the top rail from the average take-off point. This is approximately 4ft (1.2m) in front of the fence. Stand back and decide if the height is appropriate. The height of the top rail is adjusted by changing the height of the support post.

- Rope the rails to the posts.

- Trim the tops of the posts and the ends of the rails. The ends of the posts and rails are then chamfered (rounded).

CHAPTER 8 | **MAINSTAY FENCES**

## CONSTRUCTION METHOD (VERSION 2)

- Set posts in the ground at a 60° angle. Back braces will be required if the holes are less than 3ft (90cm) deep.

- Take the largest of the three logs. Wire it to the base of the posts.

- Stack the remaining two logs on top of the ground-line log. Cut spacer blocks to separate the logs. It is safer to have a solid ramp of logs if there is a drop on the landing side. The advantage of this type of construction is that it is easy to adjust the height and the post hole can be shallow so long as the post is braced.

- To avoid a potentially dangerous (4–6in/10–15cm) gap between the rails, the middle rail can be lowered, resulting in a wider gap above and a narrower gap (or no gap) below.

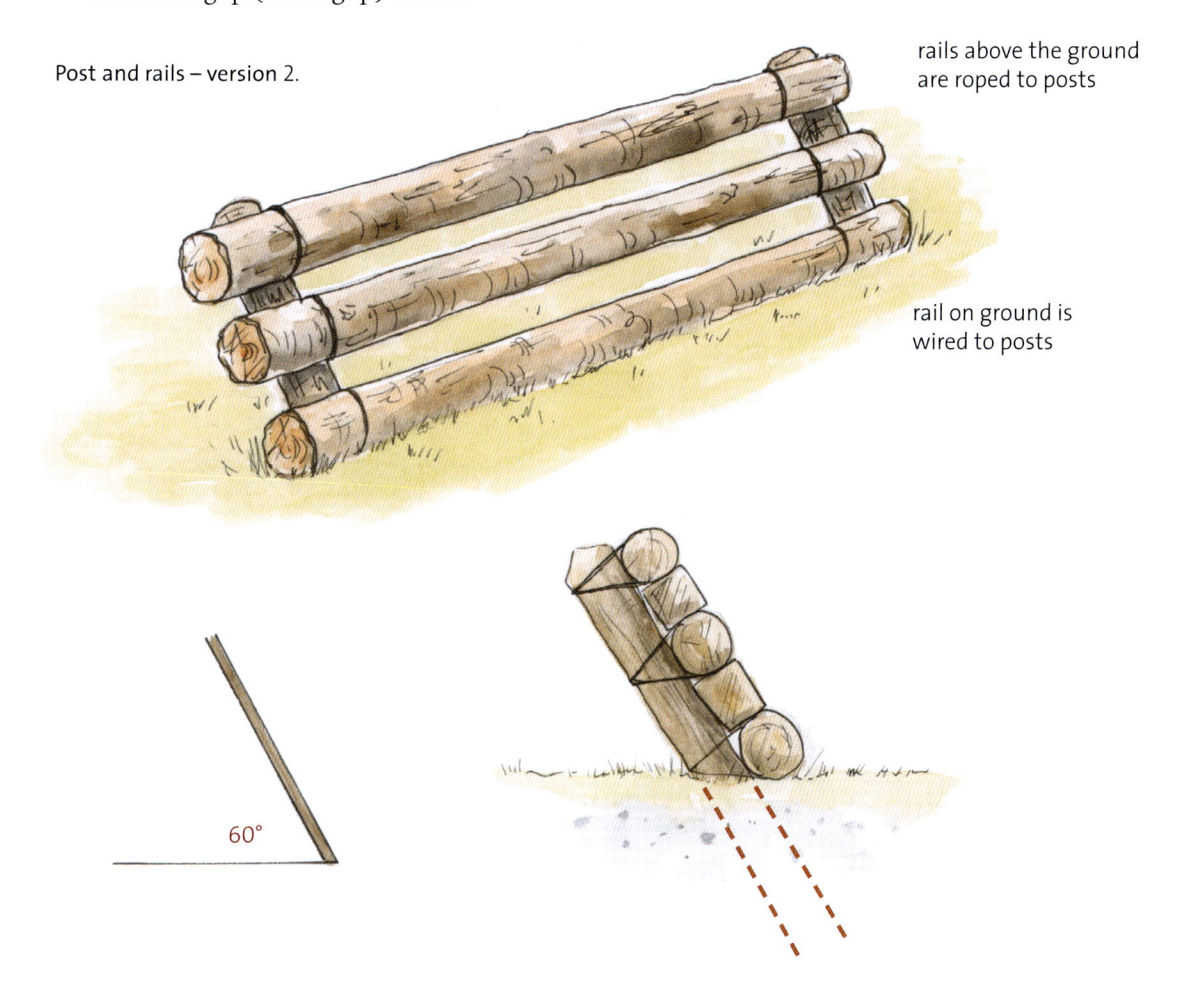

Post and rails – version 2.

rails above the ground are roped to posts

rail on ground is wired to posts

60°

53

## TIPS

- If there are problems digging the holes, see Chapter 12, on challenges. Post-hole drivers and augers enable the job to be done quickly. Digging by hand is generally necessary when the conditions are difficult or when accuracy is critical.

- Packing posts with gravel helps to prevent them from being pushed up by frost. If frost heave is a problem, then it is a good idea to point the posts. They can then be pushed back into the ground with a front-end loader.

- A 5ft (1.5m) digging bar with a chisel shape on one end and a flattened mushroom shape on the other end is an essential piece of equipment. Posts must be aggressively tamped. The ability to set posts so that they are immovable is one of the cardinal skills of the professional builder. The quality of the workmanship, or lack of it, becomes evident over time.

- Remember: you will save a lot of time if the fence height is decided before construction, so that your timber has to be cut only once. Use a mason's line to represent the top rail and give a visual reference.

- A post and rails jump with a convex face is laid out by using a 100ft (30m) tape measure as the radius of a circle. The posts will be on the circumference of the circle and at equal increments apart. The radius will be decided by trial and error, try 20ft (6m) to start.

- Rails should be at least 8in (20cm) in diameter, 10in (25cm) is better. The tops of posts and the ends of rails should be rounded or chamfered. The trick to rounding the end of posts and rails is to use the top side of the chainsaw bar for posts and the lower side of the chainsaw bar for rails. This results in a smooth cut rather than whiskers.

- It is better to wire, rather than rope, the ground rail. Field mice like rope! ⅜in (10mm) diameter nylon rope is best; polyester is the second choice; polypropylene is the cheapest and decays the quickest in sunlight.

Parallel rails or oxer.

## Parallel rails or oxer

These are straightforward fences and similar in construction to tables and farm shelters. They consist of ascending rails in front and a gap to a single back rail. It is essential that the size of the spread is obvious to a galloping horse. Having the back rail at least 2in (5cm) higher than the top front rail achieves this. Because these are open fences, it is important that they look massive and imposing; this encourages bold jumping. The rails should be 10in (25cm) in diameter. These jumps must not look airy, an oxer that is 3ft 6in (1.05m) or more in height, will probably require three rails for the front face.

### MATERIALS

- 4 logs @ 16ft–18ft (4.8m–5.4m) long and 10in (25cm) diameter (rails)
- 6 posts @ 8ft (2.4m) long and 8in (20cm) diameter (posts and support blocks for rails)
- 15ft (4.5m) of nylon rope
- 6ft (1.8m) of mild steel wire and handful of 1½in (35mm) staples

DESIGN AND BUILD A **CROSS-COUNTRY COURSE**

## CONSTRUCTION METHOD

- First build the ascending front rails (see instructions for ascending post and rails, page 53). It is easier, and looks better, to angle the posts rather than have vertical posts and accompanying support posts.

- When the front rails are built, use a 4ft (1.2m) level to determine where the post holes for the back posts will be. This is necessary to ensure the top spread dimension is correct. To do this, attach one end of the tape measure to the front of the top rail; the level is held vertically so that you can transfer the top spread measurement to the spot on the ground where the front of the back post will be.

- The top rails should be substantial to encourage bold jumping. Use the level to check that the back rail is at least 2in (5cm) higher than the front rail.

- Place the back rail on the supports that are wired to the back posts. Check the dimensions of the jump and make any necessary adjustments.

extent of top spread clearly apparent to galloping horse

ascending profile

60°

Ascending oxer.

56

- Rope the rails to the posts.
- Trim the ends of the rails and any sharp knots on the rails.

> **TIPS**
> 
> - It is easier to dig the post holes vertically and then dig out the top of one side of the hole, rather than trying to dig at an angle, although augers can be angled a few degrees.
> 
> - When setting angled posts, stand back and view them from the side before packing the fill back in. This ensures that they are at the same angle. The tendency for angled rails to lean over time can be avoided by having the holes at least 3ft (90cm) deep and if necessary, tamp flat rocks behind the posts.
> 
> - Oxers are useful filler fences. It is worth considering building them as portables. The instructions for a portable oxer are outlined in Chapter 7.
> 
> - The question asked by oxers, tables and farm shelters is very similar. If big timbers are not available consider changing the design to a table or shelter. These can be built using a sub-frame of lighter timber.

## Table

Imagine an ascending oxer with a planked top. It may not look like a traditional table, but it will ride much better. There have been problems with table jumps in the past and it is important to know the current rules and guidelines concerning their construction. The key points are that the top spread is obvious to a galloping horse, the top can be banked, it is not airy in front and it has an ascending profile. The proportions of jumps must be right. When the top spread is near maximum then the base spread should also be prominent. The back rail is at least 2in (5cm) higher than the front top rail and the front face should have a substantial amount of timber in it. When built correctly these are ideal filler fences and confidence builders.

DESIGN AND BUILD A **CROSS-COUNTRY COURSE**

Table. *(Photo: Charlotte Harper)*

## MATERIALS

4 logs @ 16ft–18ft (4.8m–5.4m) long and 10in (25cm) diameter (two top rails and two front rails)

6 posts @ 8ft (2.4m) long and 8in (20cm) diameter (posts and support posts for rails)

12 planks @ 2in x 6in (5cm x 15cm) pressure-treated or hardwood (table top)

15ft (4.5m) nylon rope

6ft (1.8m) mild steel wire and handful of 1 ½ in (35mm) staples

15lbs (7kg) of 4in (10cm) nails

## CONSTRUCTION METHOD

- To build a table jump is really simple. Follow the instructions for building an oxer and then plank the top. The planks should be countersunk into the top rails. This looks neater and gives the jump a rounded top face. The planks must be strong enough to support a horse banking the jump. Two-inch (5cm)

CHAPTER 8 | **MAINSTAY FENCES**

*3in (75mm) difference in height between front and back top spread*

*2in (5cm) thick hardwood plank*

*5°–10° from horizontal*

*60°*

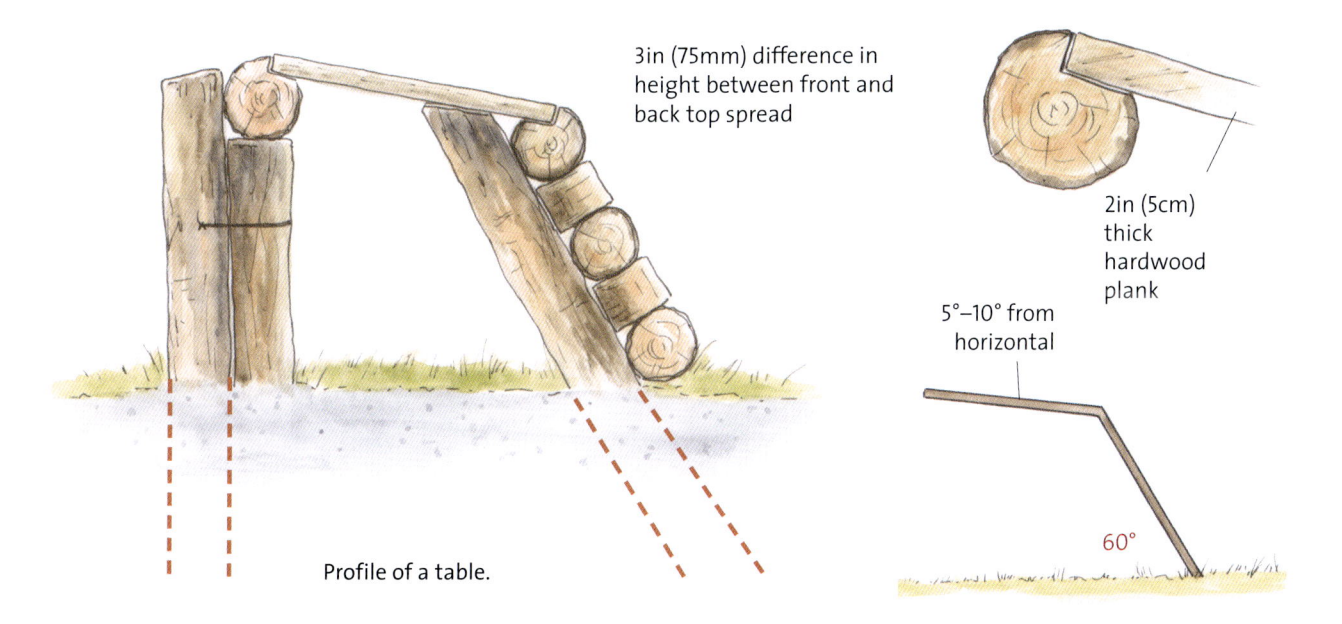

Profile of a table.

thick oak is generally adequate. If in doubt a sub-frame will have to be built to give the top extra support.

- The front consists of three ascending logs of approximately 10in (25cm) diameter. They are roped to the insides of the angled front posts. This is one of those jumps to build when big timber is available. If the diameter of the timber is too small, then consider building a farm shelter. These can have support braces on the inside and out of sight.

### TIPS

Countersinking the planks for the top requires a good eye and skill. I find that a tight mason's line is a more visible guide than a chalk one. There are many instances in course building that require advanced chainsaw skills – cutting the channel for countersunk planks is one of them. The learning curve with chainsaws is as steep as it is dangerous. If the planks are not countersunk, then they will need to be trimmed at an angle and rasped so that there are no sharp edges.

DESIGN AND BUILD A **CROSS-COUNTRY COURSE**

## Farm shelters

These are useful filler fences and come in a variety of styles. Because farm shelters are so inviting they are often used early on in a course to set horses up for the bigger spread fences. There are two main styles: the pheasant feeder and lamb creep, both of which have a gable roof (like a house), and the shed-roofed shelter (like a lean-to). The shed-roofed shelter has an ascending front face and is open on the opposite side. Both types are simple to construct; the only challenge is in fitting the roof so that it does not have a protruding sharp edge. Countersinking the lower edge of the roof into the log supporting it does this. Brush-covered straw bales or shrubs can be used to fill the gap between the ground and the roof.

Gable-roofed farm shelter.

flowers or shrubs for groundline

detail of roof showing smooth rounded edged

lap joint at end posts

## MATERIALS

> 3 logs @ 16ft–18ft (4.8m–5.4m) and 10in (25cm) diameter (ridgepole and back and front frame for roof)
>
> 12 posts @ 7ft (2.1m) and 8in (20cm) diameter (support for roof)
>
> 12–18 planks @ 2in x 6in (5cm x 15cm) pressure-treated or hardwood (for roof)
>
> 12 nails @ 10in (25cm) or 12in (30cm), or 15ft (4.5m) of 9-gauge wire and handful of 1½in (35mm) staples
>
> 15lbs (7kg) of 4in (100mm) nails

## CONSTRUCTION METHOD

- To build a gabled-roof shelter the first step is to mark out the rectangular shape on the ground with a mason's line. Measure the diagonals to ensure that the corners are square. Mark each post hole. Generally there are double the number of posts than are structurally required; this helps fill in the front and back faces of the jump.

- Set the corner posts first and fasten a line around them – this serves as a guide to ensure that the remaining posts are in line. Set the remainder of the posts.

- The two centre posts on either end will support the ridgepole, and the two pairs of posts at either end will support the frame that forms the lower edge of the roof.

- The joints at the end posts could be either an open tenon and mortise joint or the easier lap joints.

- Cut a quarter section channel out of the logs that form the front and back frame so that the planks are countersunk into the rails.

- Plank the roof. The timbers must be strong enough to support a horse banking the jump. The ends of the shelter can be planked and trimmed with fascia board, if desired, for a more finished appearance.

- The shed roof shelter is simpler to build. Build an oxer and then plank the roof and take-off side. Using half-rounds instead of planks results in a more

DESIGN AND BUILD A **CROSS-COUNTRY COURSE**

Rustic farm shelter.

Rear view. *(Photo: Charlotte Harper)*

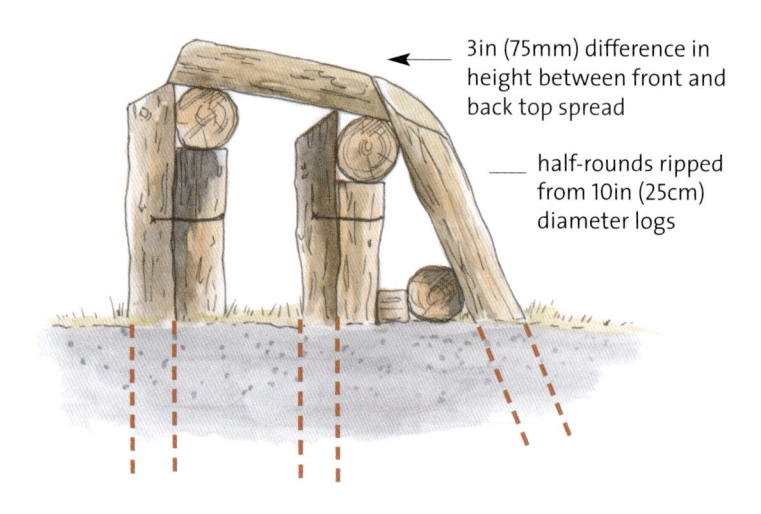

← 3in (75mm) difference in height between front and back top spread

___ half-rounds ripped from 10in (25cm) diameter logs

62

CHAPTER 8 | **MAINSTAY FENCES**

Shed-roofed farm shelter.

roof countersunk into front top log

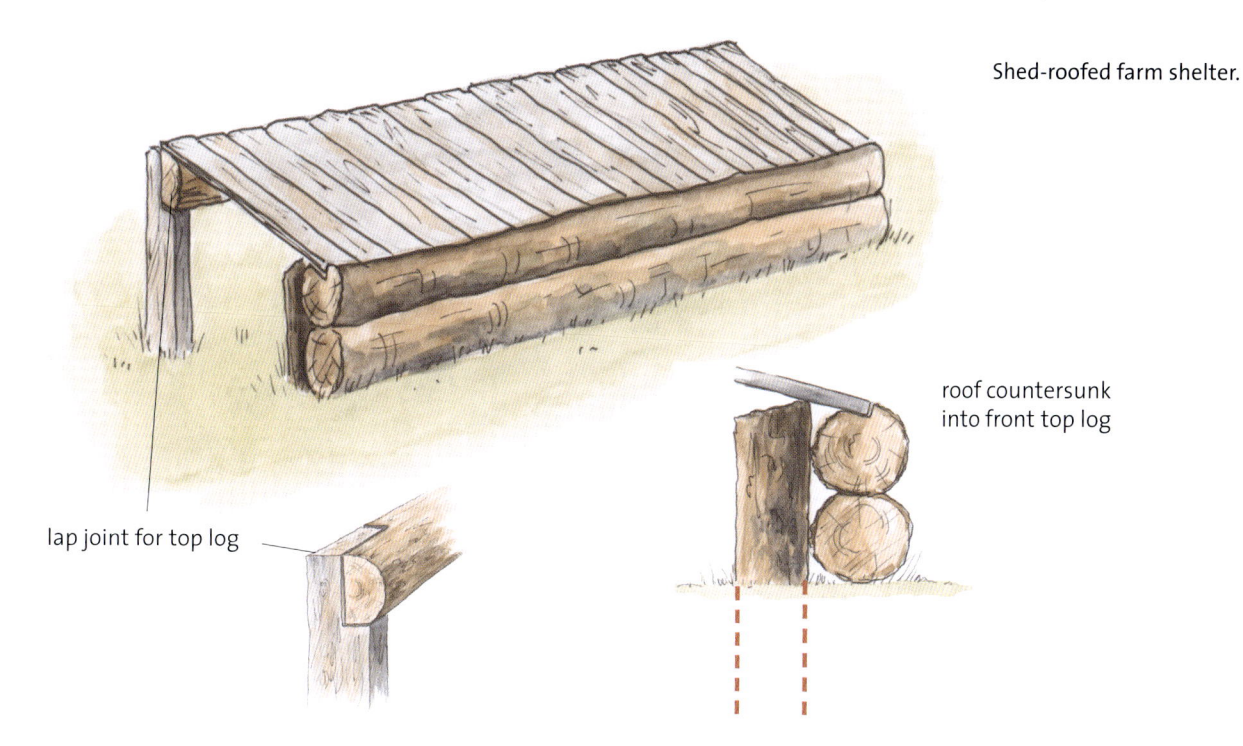

lap joint for top log

rustic looking shelter. If half-rounds are used, they should not be less than 6in (150mm) thick.

- An interesting alternative is to have a brick roof. The bricks are supported by ¾in (20mm) exterior plywood. The logs will need to be 10in (25cm) in diameter because a deeper channel is required so that the bricks are flush with the front and top log.

## Ski ramp

Ski ramps are very straightforward to build and fun to ride. The two critical aspects are the angle of the ramp and how the jump is sited in relation to the drop. Drop fences put wear and tear on horses' legs. At the lower levels of competition the drop should be largely an illusion. Site the fence back far enough from the edge of the slope so that the horse will land before the ground drops away. Rules cannot cover every situation and deciding on the dimensions of fences on sloping ground depends on good judgement. A ski ramp can be built with the timber in a horizontal or vertical plane. This will depend on the length and strength of the available construction material. For example: railway sleepers will be horizontal, and oak planks vertical.

# DESIGN AND BUILD A CROSS-COUNTRY COURSE

Ski ramp with horizontal timbers, built with railway sleepers.

two upper sleepers roped and two lower sleepers wired to posts

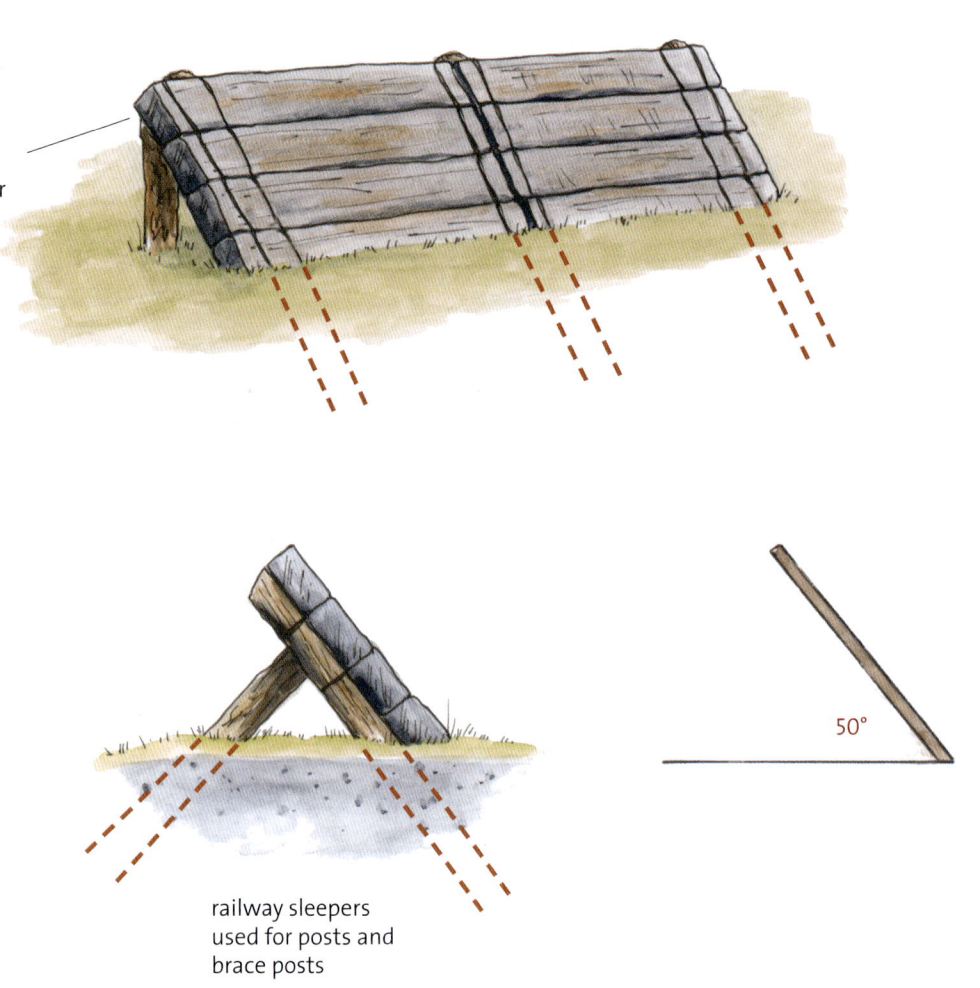

railway sleepers used for posts and brace posts

50°

## MATERIALS

11–13 railway sleepers (ties), or alternatively 3 posts 8ft/2.4m long and 8in/20cm diameter, 2 logs (16ft/4.8m) and 12 planks @ 2in x 6in (5cm x 15cm) and 12ft/3.6m long. Railway sleepers can be fastened with wire, rope or nails; planks with 4in (10cm) or 5in (12.5cm) nails.

## CONSTRUCTION METHOD

- Carefully choose the best site, bearing in mind that it should only appear to be a leap into space.

CHAPTER 8 | **MAINSTAY FENCES**

- The soil is thinnest on hilltops, so digging a 4ft (1.2m) post hole may not be feasible. This is not critical as the brace posts support the structure.

- Approximately 50° is the best angle for the ramp.

- Dig the post holes and set the posts at an angle. It may be necessary to have a centre post. Brace the posts.

- If the jump is being faced with upright planks rather than sleepers, then a top and bottom rail will be wired to the posts. The planks are then nailed onto the rails. If building with horizontal rails or sleepers, place them in position and then stand back to assess the height. The easiest way to adjust the height is to dig in the lowest rail.

- Measure the height from the anticipated take-off point and then measure the drop. A ski ramp is one of those fences that you have to stand back and have a good look at it. Trust your intuition as to whether or not the dimensions are appropriate.

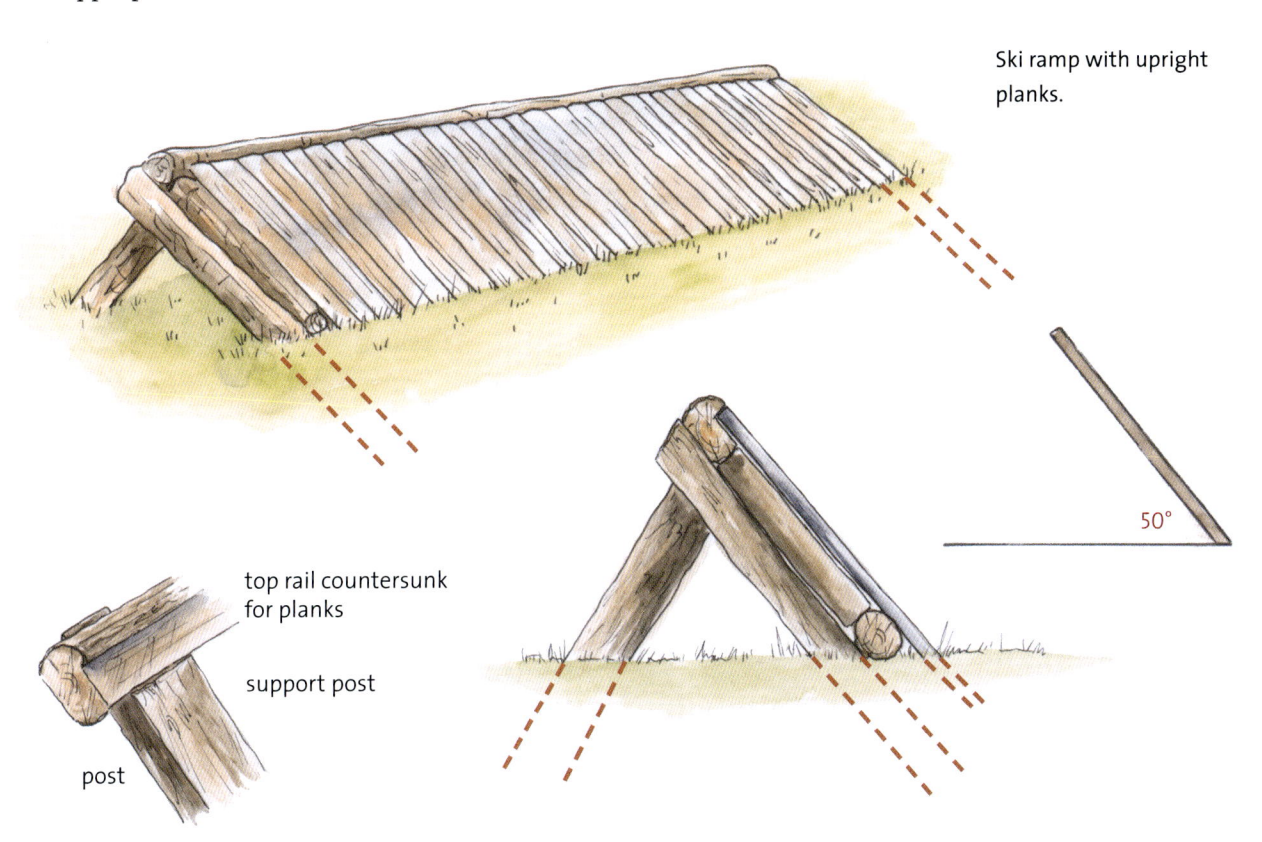

Ski ramp with upright planks.

50°

top rail countersunk for planks

support post

post

## Steeplechase and brush fences

These are the ideal fences to inspire confidence and big jumping. I like to put one early in the course as a stretching exercise before the more serious efforts to come. The only downside with these fences is the amount of brush it takes to stuff them. The construction is straightforward and it is virtually the same for all levels of competition. Packing the brush is time-consuming and finicky, but the final look of the fence depends upon the diligence with which the greenery is packed. Brush jumps either have a roll of brush – called an apron – as a ground-line, or an open ditch. Both tell the horses where to take off. A substantial ground rail hides the ditch from a galloping horse, but looks impressive when viewed from the side.

### MATERIALS

> 3 logs @ 16ft (4.8m) long and 10in (25cm) diameter (two are ripped into half-rounds, the other is a ground-line)
>
> 2 posts @ 6ft (1.8m) and 8in (20cm) diameter or 6in x 6in (15cm x 15cm) (posts for frame and ground rail)
>
> 2 posts @ 4ft (1.2m) and 8in (20cm) diameter or 6in x 6in (15cm x 15cm) (for brace posts)

Steeplechase fence.

CHAPTER 8 | **MAINSTAY FENCES**

> 1 or 2 full wagon-loads of brush, and 12 straw bales for the apron
>
> 6ft (1.8m) of nylon rope
>
> 5lbs (2.5kg) of 8in (20cm) nails
>
> 6ft (1.8m) of mild steel wire and handful of 1½in (35mm) staples

## CONSTRUCTION METHOD

- Set a pair of 6ft (1.8m) posts in the ground 16ft (4.8m) apart. For a regular steeplechase fence these should be set at an 80° angle. This helps with the ascending profile. In some situations the posts are vertical and the apron or ditch gives the fence an ascending profile.

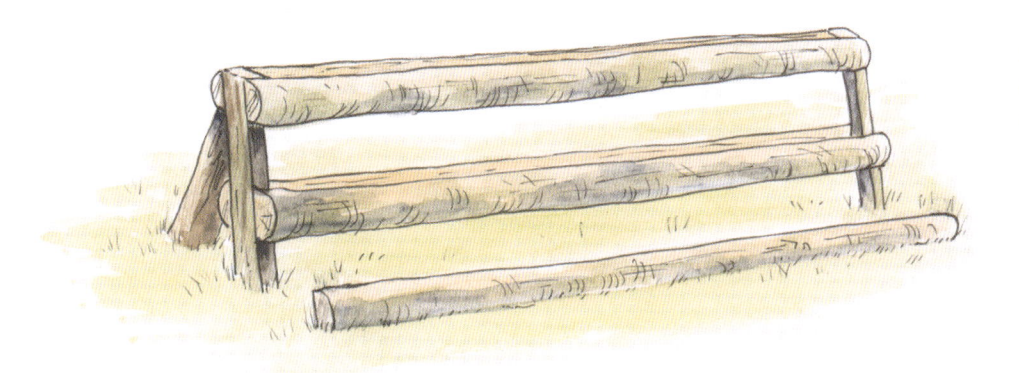

Steeplechase frame prior to roping and packing brush

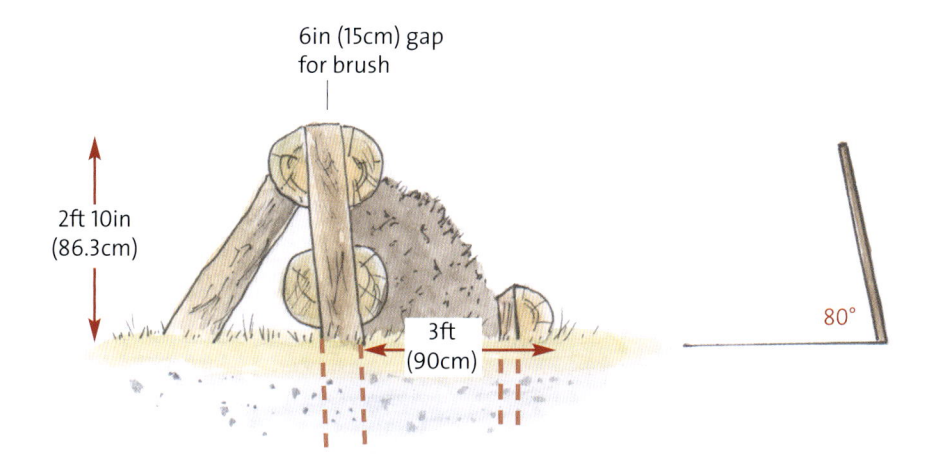

6in (15cm) gap for brush

2ft 10in (86.3cm)

3ft (90cm)

80°

67

- Rip two 16ft (4.8m) rails (not less than 8in/20cm diameter) into half-rounds.

- The top of the frame will be 2ft 10in (86.3cm) high. Mark this on the posts.

- Nail and then rope a half-round to both the front and the back of the post.

- The top of the half-round will be at the 2ft 10in (86.3cm) mark.

- Repeat for the lower pair of half-rounds. The top of these should be approximately 12in (30cm) off the ground. It is prudent to have one or two brace posts supporting the top half-round on the landing side.

- The ground rail should be substantial and clearly visible. It is positioned 3ft (90cm) in front of the frame and is either staked or held in place by a timber that is nailed to the post. The ground rail is closer to the frame if the height of the brush is under 4ft (1.2m).

- Lay the brush out and trim off the thick ends so that each bough will be 6in (15cm) taller than the finished height of the jump. Packing the frame with brush that is only slightly longer than the height of the fence reduces the number of thick, sharp spikes.

- Pack the brush in the frame. It takes a prodigious amount of material to stuff a fence – roughly twice what one would anticipate. The thicker boughs stiffen the back of the frame and the smaller pieces green up the front. It is important to pack the brush so that it naturally leans toward the landing side of the fence. It must be dense enough so that there is no possibility of a horse dropping a leg between the frame.

- Trim the brush to the desired height. Trimming it at an angle helps create the ascending profile. Search for sharp spikes and cut them right back. Fill any gaps with sprigs and trim again.

- The roll of brush (or apron) must be solid enough to withstand a horse stepping on it. Tightly packed straw bales with a covering of brush is one solution. A prominent ground rail encourages clean jumping.

## Garden frame

Garden frames are ideal fences for either the beginning or the end of the course. They are like a book cover and frame the drama with a splash of colour. These are ornamental fences and some thought should go into their construction – they should not look like an afterthought one might see at some forgotten railway station. Construction methods and materials vary, but the end result is a raised flower bed in a wooden or fieldstone frame. There are two main building styles: the first one consists of a substantial frame that will support three feet of topsoil, while the other one has a lighter frame built out of milled lumber and has a false top. Both methods have their advantages; it comes down to the material and equipment that is available.

These are decorative fences and it is worth using materials that are pleasing to the eye. Railway ties and pressure-treated lumber are structurally ideal, but they do have that unfortunate 'timber yard' look. Instead, consider building a log-cabin style frame using rustic logs with a saddle notch tying the logs together, or better still, square beams with dovetail joins.

Fieldstone always looks great – budget and availability of stone permitting. The stones should be substantial in size and the principles of dry stone wall construction followed. If stone is used, a prominent top rail is necessary to ensure that the jump is horse-friendly.

For the upper levels of competition the profile should be similar to that of any fence with substantial height and top spread. This can be achieved by having a smaller flowerbed in front. This serves as a ground-line.

### MATERIALS

7 logs @ 16ft–18ft (4.8m–5.4m) and 10in (25cm) diameter (frame and top log)

6 logs @ 4ft (1.2m) and 10in (25cm) diameter (frame)

Logs for frame can be fastened by notches, nails or steel rods; top log with rope

DESIGN AND BUILD A **CROSS-COUNTRY COURSE**

Garden frame with half-round top, front and back. The fieldstone framed garden in front makes the jump more ascending.

This garden frame (or flower box) with a suspended log over the centre, can be ridden from either direction. It is possible to make this fence a portable one.
(Photo: Charlotte Harper)

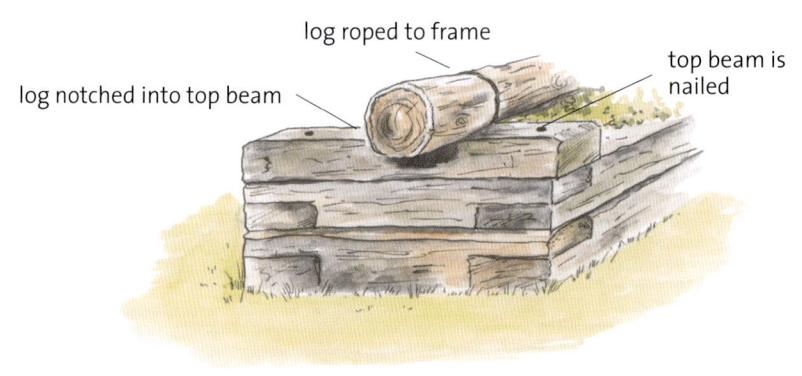

log roped to frame
top beam is nailed
log notched into top beam

CHAPTER 8 | **MAINSTAY FENCES**

## CONSTRUCTION METHOD

- A flower box can be built to ride from either direction. To do this, suspend a log over the centre. This works well for the lower levels – in this case the dimensions of the frame might be 4ft (1.2m) wide and 2ft (60cm) high. The top log brings the height to approximately 3ft (90cm).

- As for the flowers, the simplest, and arguably the best looking, is to plant some perennial creeping ground cover and then add bright synthetic flowers for the competition. Local landscape companies are often happy to loan plants and shrubs in return for free advertising.

- A trellis archway over the jump is another nice touch, and is simple to do. The archway will need to give 12ft (3.6m) clearance above the ground. Hanging flower baskets are another decorative idea. These can hang from a light curved pole, 8ft (2.4m) high. The poles are nailed to either end of the fence.

- A frame built out of milled lumber must have a deck that is strong enough for a horse to bank off it. This is done by building a sub-frame supported by posts. The timber must be exterior grade.

## Sharks' teeth

Sharks' teeth, also known as chevrons, have three useful attributes: they look different, ride well and their construction is simple. The jump is made up of two or more chevrons supported by a back rail. The pointed end of the chevron is

Sharks' teeth, with planks. *(Photo: Charlotte Harper)*

DESIGN AND BUILD A **CROSS-COUNTRY COURSE**

Sharks' teeth, without planks.

dug into the ground approximately 3ft (90cm) in front of the fence. Dressing the gaps between the teeth is necessary to prevent the fence looking too airy. Flowers, an ornamental shrub or even a small boulder will do the job. The gap between the arms of the chevrons (both top and bottom) must be at least 6in (15cm). This is to prevent the possibility of a horse's leg getting caught in the vee. The 'teeth' or chevrons can be either left open or planked; generally at the lower levels they are planked. A sharks' teeth fence is useful when you want a challenge without a big jumping effort – for example, as the first element of a coffin.

### MATERIALS

1 log @ 16ft (4.8m) long and 10in (25cm) diameter

3 posts @ 8ft (2.4m) and 8in (20cm) diameter (2 posts for top rails and supports for rail)

4 half rounds @ 6ft (1.8m) and 10in (20cm) diameter

CHAPTER 8 | **MAINSTAY FENCES**

- 8 planks @ 12ft (3.6m) and 2in x 6in (5cm x 15cm)
- 5lbs (2.5kg) of 8in (20cm) nails
- 10lbs (5kg) of 4in (10cm) nails
- 6ft (1.8m) of nylon rope
- 6ft (1.8m) of mild steel wire and handful of 1½in (35mm) staples

## CONSTRUCTION METHOD

- Building the support frame for the chevrons is straightforward. Set two posts 14ft (4.2m) apart. The top rail rests on support posts. These are wired to the posts in the ground. The height of the rail is at least 2in (5cm) lower than the maximum top height for the level of competition. For the lower levels, a pair of 'teeth' is all that is necessary and these will fit on a 14ft (4.2m) rail. A 16ft (4.8m) wide fence requires three chevrons.

- The construction challenge is to build it so that the 'teeth' are straight. Measure the distance between the posts and mark the centre-point of the top rail. Mark 4in (10cm) inside the ends of the rail and 4in (10cm) either side of the centre-point. These marks will be the top edges of the chevrons. Then mark the centre of the top of both chevrons.

- Make a mark on the ground 3ft (90cm) in front of the centre of both chevrons. This is where the point of each chevron will be. The hole to take the point is 1ft (30cm) deep and 2ft (60cm) wide. The measurements and symmetry have to be exact. Accurate measuring helps but you will still need to stand back and view the jump from a distance before deciding the angle and position of the chevron frame.

- The two pairs of timbers that support the planks are 8in (20cm) diameter half-round 6ft (1.8m) long. They will need to be trimmed at the point so that they fit tight together and flush with the top rail. When you are satisfied that the angles are all correct, then nail the top of the half-rounds to the rail. The hole that takes the points is then filled and well tamped. A useful trick is to hold a 16ft (4.8m) plank against the timbers forming the teeth to ensure that they are all in the same plane.

- The top of the chevron will be approximately 6ft (1.8m) wide. Nail the planks to the half-rounds. To prevent there being a small gap between the top plank and the rail it is necessary for the plank to be an inch (25mm) higher than the rail. If necessary, the fence can be lowered after construction by cutting a slice off the top rail support posts. It is easiest to nail the top plank first and work down. The lowest plank can be partially buried in the ground.

- Ornamental shrubs should be planted in the gaps between the chevrons. If shrubs are not feasible, a moss-covered boulder will do the job.

- If the fence is for the lower levels of competition then a ground rail across the front of the fence will make it more inviting. The points of the chevrons are nailed to it. Conversely the jump can be made more difficult by not planking the chevrons.

## Cordwood

From a builder's viewpoint the advantage of these jumps is that they can be constructed out of second-rate material. The downside is that they do require a prodigious amount of timber. These jumps are ideal for gaps in fence-lines, when rocks and roots discourage digging. A ground-rail log in front and a top back rail achieve the ascending profile. The construction is straightforward; it is little more than a stack of short logs held in place by end posts. Rails on top help to hold it all together and give it a rounded top edge.

Cordwood.

CHAPTER 8 | **MAINSTAY FENCES**

## MATERIALS

- 3 logs @ 16ft (4.8m) and 9in–10in (23cm–25cm) diameter (top rails and ground rail)

- 2 logs @ 16ft (4.8m) and 4in–6in (10–15cm) (to lift cordwood off the ground to delay rotting)

- 4 posts @ 8ft (2.4m) and 8in (20cm) diameter (posts)

- Stack of logs approx. 4ft x 4ft x 16ft (1.2m x 1.2m x 4.8m)

- 12ft (3.5m) of 9- or 10-gauge mild steel wire and handful of 1½in (35mm) staples

## CONSTRUCTION METHOD

- Place the two 16ft (4.8m) (4in–6in/10–15cm) rails on the ground. These rails help reduce the amount of timber and make it easier to trim the cordwood.

- Set a post at each of the four corners of the proposed cordwood. If the two posts at each end are angled toward each other, then the two top rails will be easier to fit.

- Cut the logs for the cordwood to the exact length and place them evenly between the posts, laid on the 4in–6in (10–15cm) logs so they are off the ground. The more even and uniform these logs, the better the jump will look.

- Mark on the posts the top height of the fence. Build the cordwood up to the height of the bottom of the top rails.

Side view of cordwood showing construction detail.

- The front top rail should be a smaller diameter than the back rail. Place these rails on the top of the cordwood. The front rail will be in front of the posts, while the back rail will be behind the back posts. Wire both ends of the rails together and twist the wire to draw the rails tight to the posts. Staple the wire to the posts.

- The gap between the rails is filled with logs of a similar diameter to the rails.

- The front top edge of the cordwood will need to be trimmed off at an angle to create a more rounded profile. A log is placed on the ground in front of the fence and wired to the front post. It is the size of this ground rail and the difference in height between the front and back top rails that gives the fence its ascending profile.

### TIPS

- Used fence posts and other recycled timbers are ideal cordwood material, as are rails whose small diameter makes them unsuitable for other jumps.

- If there is not enough timber, then have only one or two layers of cordwood and make up the height with rails stacked on the logs.

- The logs are held in place by tightly packing smaller logs between the top layer and the rails. However, it may be necessary to nail the logs together.

## Log cabins

Log cabins can turn a combination into an eye-catching work of art. Cutting the notches is much easier than it looks and for novice cabin builders, a few minor mistakes are not that critical. This is after all a jump, not a shelter from arctic blizzards. A cross-country course should reflect the heritage of the region and incorporate traditional building methods whenever possible. Depending on the locality, cabins are a way of achieving this. The simplest type of log cabin is built from logs with a saddle notch. The next step up is to use logs that have been squared into beams and held together with dovetail joins. The external

CHAPTER 8 | **MAINSTAY FENCES**

Log cabin built with barn beams and dovetail joints.

appearance may resemble a traditional cabin but obviously there are modifications to fit the requirements of it being a jump. Other traditional building methods and materials to consider are: adobe, thatch and sod-roofed cabins, and fieldstone buildings. Artistic flair should not subjugate the requirements of the horse.

## MATERIALS

5 logs or squared beams @ 16ft (4.8m) and 10in (25cm) diameter (front and back sides and ridge pole)

4 logs or beams @ 4ft (1.2m) and 10in (25cm) diameter (left and right hand ends of cabin)

12–14 planks @ 12ft (3.6m) long and 2in x 6in (5cm x 15cm) (roof)

15lbs (7kg) of 4in (10cm) nails

## CONSTRUCTION METHOD

- Begin the construction with the long logs at the front and back of the cabin. It is prudent to have the width of the cabin within the maximum top spread dimension for that level of competition.

- Place two short logs on top of the front and back logs. Check the width and

Dovetail joins.

wedge cut from lower beam is same dimension as wedge cut from upper log

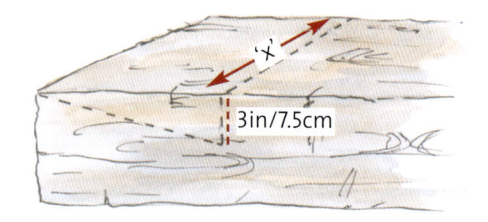

10in/25cm

3in/7.5cm

3in/7.5cm

Detail of dovetail joins with beams.

Detail of dovetail joins with rounded logs.

measure the diagonals to ensure that the frame is square. The end logs should extend 12in (30cm) beyond the sides. This allows you to modify and adjust the width of the cabin during construction. However, when the frame is built, all the protruding ends of the logs should be evenly trimmed back so that they are not a potential hazard.

- Use a lumber crayon to mark the outline of the curve (or notch for the dovetail) of the upper log onto the log beneath it. (If using logs, the basic idea is to duplicate the circumference of the upper log onto the lower log). A pair of dividers or scribes helps with accuracy, but it can be done by eye. Repeat this for all four corners. The depth of the notch is approximately a third of the diameter of the log. Both ends of the log are marked before cutting. If you are building a house the notch is cut out of the upper log, but for a jump it is easier to cut the notch out of the lower one.

- Cut out the notch and round it off so that the upper log will fit snugly.

- Do the same for the end logs.

- Repeat the procedure until you have the frame for a cabin that is two layers of logs high. The ridgepole and the planked roof are what hold it all together. The planks for the roof are countersunk into the top log of the wall.

- The gaps between the logs can be 'chinked' (filled with mortar). A cabin with 2in (5cm) gaps will require six bags of mortar mix. The mortar is held in place by nailing strips of fine-mesh chicken wire in the gaps. A field-stone chimney at one end of the cabin adds to the look of authenticity.

- If the height has to be adjusted after construction it is not too difficult to either raise or dig in the cabin by adjusting the height of the bottom log.

- To build a bigger cabin, use more layers of logs.

> **TIP**
>
> Building with dovetail joins is deceptively easy. The trick is to have a sharp lumber crayon so that the cuts are accurate. A wedge is cut out of either end of the beam. The thick end of the wedge is 3in (7.5cm) deep and this is cut out of the inside of the end of the beam. A similar wedge is cut out of the upper beam. The wedges that are going to be cut from all four corners, both lower and upper beams, are measured and marked with crayon before any are cut. If the joins are uneven, either take the beams apart and lightly trim the join, or carefully run the chainsaw between the join. The ridgepole and planked roof lock the structure together.

## Stone wall

There are three things on a cross-country course that are pleasing to the eye – green brush, water and natural field-stone. In fact, you should take every opportunity to get away from the look of rails and logs. There are two requirements for a good stone wall – plenty of rocks and an appreciation of how to make gravity work for you. A 16ft (4.8m) wall, 3ft 6in (1.05m) high, has roughly 12 cubic yds/m of material – which is a tandem-axle dump-truck load. Cement and foundations are only mankind's way of delaying the effects of gravity and it is worth noting that a well-built stone wall will outlast many engineered structures. The key point is to cross every join, and to have the rocks leaning in toward the centre. Choose rocks that have a rectangular or irregular shape; old foundations, buildings and hedgerows are a good source of material. the top of the fence must be capped with timber; if the spread is noticeable it should have both a front and back rail (as shown below).

### MATERIALS

- 1 or 2 logs @ 16ft (4.8m) and 10in (25cm) diameter (top rails)
- 4 posts @ 8ft (2.4m) long and 8in (20cm) diameter (support for top rails)
- 10–12 cubic yds/m of fieldstone
- 4 nails @ 12in (30cm) (fasten rail to posts)

Stone wall.

CHAPTER 8 | **MAINSTAY FENCES**

half-rounds nailed to posts

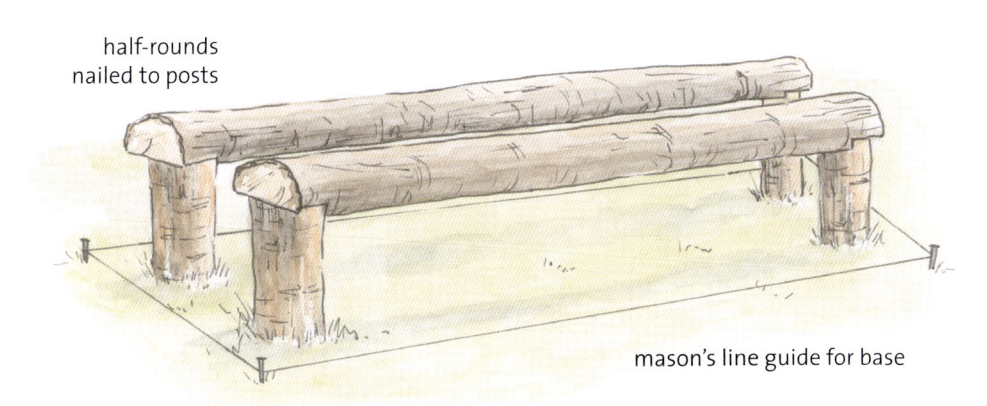

Top logs and their supports are built before the construction of the wall.

mason's line guide for base

## CONSTRUCTION METHOD

- Before deciding to build a wall, make sure that there is sufficient stone available. It is important to have more than is necessary so that you have a selection of rocks to choose from.

- The top rails, to reduce the risk of injury, should be built first. Set a post at either end of the proposed wall and position the rails on support posts that are wired to the posts. An alternative method is to use a 10in (25cm) diameter half-round and nail this directly on top of the posts.

- The base width for a 3ft 6in (1.05m) high wall should be not less than 4ft (1.2m). It is helpful to mark this out on the ground using a mason's line. The correct procedure is to remove the topsoil and replace it with gravel; this prevents the wall from settling over time. In practice it is more cost-effective to build it on top of the ground and if it does lower an inch or two over the years then a few more stones can be added. Most jumps shrink over time.

- Start by positioning the biggest, squarest rocks at each corner. Then build both sides. Use the biggest rocks or boulders in the bottom layer. This prevents having to lift them and they can also be dug in to achieve the ascending profile.

- After building each layer, fill in the middle with smaller odd-shaped stones, rubble and gravel. It is tempting to use topsoil to fill in the cracks. This is a bad practice. The soil will absorb moisture which, when it freezes, will expand and weaken the structure.

DESIGN AND BUILD A **CROSS-COUNTRY COURSE**

Dry stone wall under construction.

- Dry stone wall building is a craft and not a job to do in a hurry. It generally will take a full day to build a good-sized stone wall.

## TIPS

- The wall can be made less vertical by having a log on the ground in front. The angle of the wall is approximately 70°. Professional masons use stakes and nylon line as a guide during construction.

- Fresh grass sod on the top will help soften the look and make it more horse-friendly.

- Collecting rocks is a great way to get a work party out of your hair. But building by committee does not work.

- If there are only rounded boulders available, use them to build a rock garden with a suspended log over the top. The boulders are arranged to form the sides of a rectangle and the centre is filled with topsoil.

CHAPTER 8 | MAINSTAY FENCES

## Corner

Corner jumps are a safe way to put the emphasis on testing riders rather than horses. The hallmarks of a well-built corner are that it is well sited, ascending, and the extent of the spread is obvious. Planking the top makes corner fences considerably safer. The widest section must be made unjumpable. Planting trees or nailing evergreens at the unjumpable part of the corner achieves this. In addition, a potted shrub can be placed on the wide end of the planked top. Because these fences require accurate riding it is important that the approach is free of encumbrances such as branches or uneven ground.

### MATERIALS

- 4 logs @ 10ft (3m) long and 10in (25cm) diameter (top and front rails)
- 6 posts @ 8ft (2.4m) and 8in (20cm) diameter (posts for rails and supports for rails)
- 6 planks @ 12ft (3.6m) and 2in x 6in (5cm x 15cm) (top, strong enough to be bankable)
- 10lbs (5kg) of 4in (10cm) nails
- 15ft (4.5m) of nylon rope

Corner. For safety reasons the numbers and letters marking the point of a corner should be attached to the outside of the stake rather than centred on it, as in this photo. *(Photo: Charlotte Harper)*

83

DESIGN AND BUILD A **CROSS-COUNTRY COURSE**

## CONSTRUCTION METHOD

- Take the two top rails, place them on the ground and adjust them so that they are the correct angle apart. There have been different opinions on how to measure the top spread of a corner. The standard practice is that 4ft (1.2m) in from the point must be within the top spread dimension for that level of competition.

- Use the rails as a guide mark as to where the post hole will be dug. The post at the point is between the rails and the other two posts are behind the rails. Dig and set the posts.

- Position both top rails on their support posts. These support posts should be wired rather than nailed so that adjusting the height of the top rails is easier. The back rail must be 2–3in (5–7.5cm) higher than the front rail.

- Add two more ascending rails to the front. These are equidistant apart. The front face of the corner will now have three ascending rails. The thinnest rail

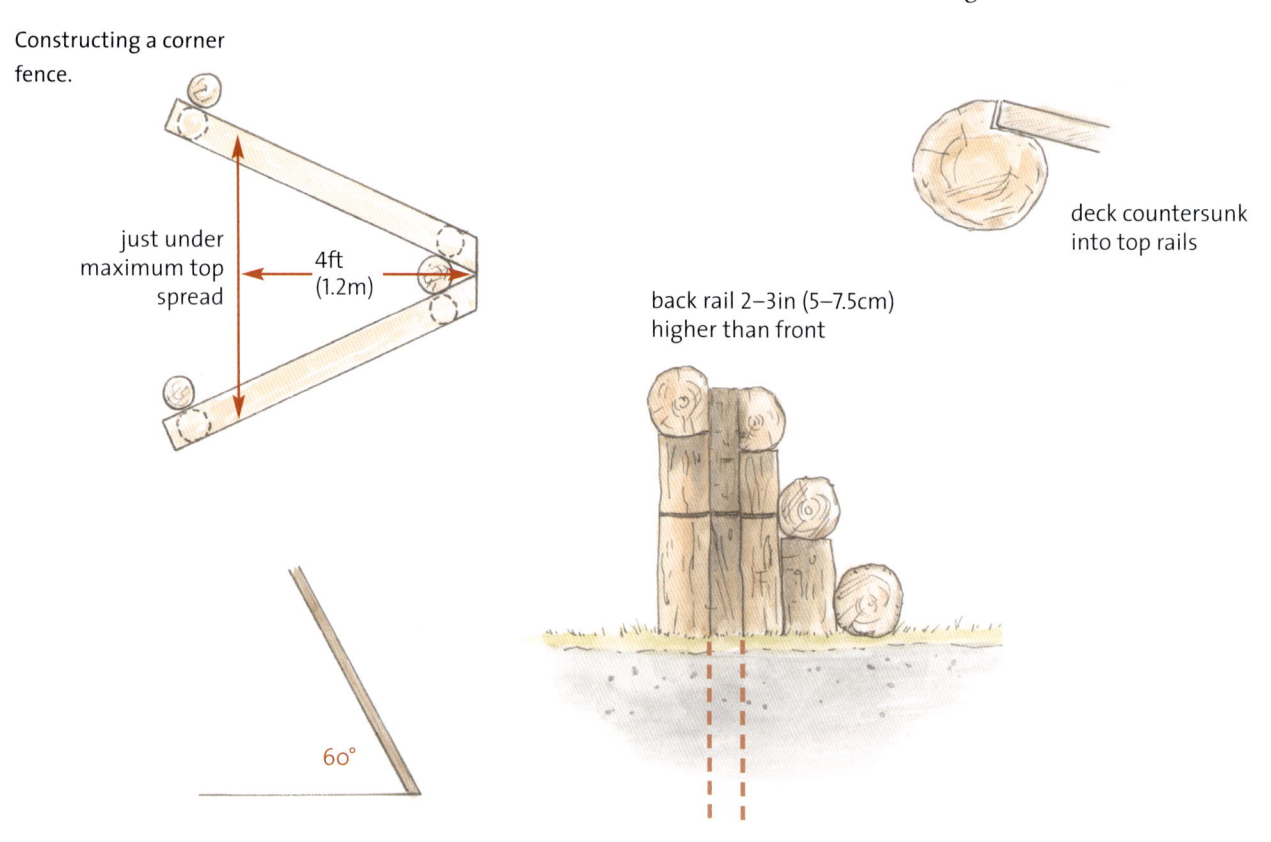

Constructing a corner fence.

just under maximum top spread

4ft (1.2m)

deck countersunk into top rails

back rail 2–3in (5–7.5cm) higher than front

60°

- is on top and the thickest on the ground. These rails should be not less than 9in (23cm) in diameter.

- The top deck is countersunk into the top rails. This should not be attempted with a chainsaw unless your skills are up to it. Use either a chalk-line or a taut nylon line as a cutting guide.

- Measure, cut and fit the planks for the deck. If you are concerned that the planks may not be strong enough, then it is simple to build a frame to support them from underneath the deck. The nailed deck will hold the top rails in position. The lower rails are roped.

- Competitors are expected either to jump the fence reasonably close to the point or have a run-out. Attempting to negotiate the widest part must be prevented. Evergreen trees planted along the widest side will do this, as will a potted shrub positioned on the widest part of the deck.

## TIPS

- Because these are challenging fences, it is important that their siting is given careful thought. Siting them on gently rising ground, four or five strides after a turn will have horses naturally collected and in a good jumping frame.

- Double corners, two strides apart (36ft/10.8m), is a good question to ask. For competitions with two or more levels, build the first corner at near maximum dimensions for the lower level of competition. The lower level jumps the first corner and the upper level jumps both. To do this requires the builder to have a good eye for a line as they have to be slightly offset.

- Organisers may request that the corner can be jumped from both directions. This is not a good idea, as there is always only one optimum site and position for a corner. However, it can be done. Build an ascending planked face on both sides and a level top deck. The extent of the spread is defined by nailing a half-round to the back of the deck. This half-round is then easy to move to the other side for a change in direction.

DESIGN AND BUILD A **CROSS-COUNTRY COURSE**

## Ditches

Ditches are an inherent part of cross-country courses. They can be used in an infinite number of ways and really make a course interesting. However, they if they are not built with skill, the results are obvious and regretted. The revetting or retaining wall must be tied back to a secure anchor and then back-filled with rock rather than topsoil. The lumber used for revetting must be suitable for contact with the ground and wet conditions. Railway sleepers (ties) or pressure-treated timber are generally the materials of choice. However, there are environmental concerns with both these materials and their use may be restricted or banned in the future. In North America, there are three species that are resistant to rot in wet conditions – Eastern white cedar, red cedar and locust. Although it is arguable which is the lesser of two evils – potential toxic leaching from preservatives, or logging healthy trees? The regulations concerning the use and contents of pressure-treated timber are frequently changing and builders should know the relevant local bye-laws. It is easy to underestimate the cost of ditches: labour, timber and gravel all add up. However, there is a simpler method of construction that can be used on dry ground for the lower levels. This method circumvents the need for tying back the sides of the ditch and is described on page 89.

Ditch with half round on take-off side. Note: ditch should be dug out 6in/15cm deeper. *(Photo: Charlotte Harper)*

CHAPTER 8 | **MAINSTAY FENCES**

## MATERIALS

16–20 railway sleepers (ties) @ 8ft (2.4m) long (sides of ditch)

or alternatively 10 pressure-treated 6in x 6in beams @ 16ft (15cm x 15cm @ 4.8m) long

3 steel fence posts @ 7ft (2.1m) (cut in half for anchor posts)

6 half-round posts @ 6ft (1.8m) long and 9in (23cm) diameter (posts)

45ft (13.5m) of 9 or 10 gauge mild steel wire (to wire front half rounds to anchor posts) and handful of 1 ½ in (35mm) staples

10lbs (5kg) of 8in (20cm) nails

## CONSTRUCTION METHOD

- Excavate 2ft (60cm) wider than the width of the finished ditch. This allows for the width of the revetting. Two feet (60cm) deep is an ideal depth – too shallow and a horse may step in it; too deep and a horse may fall in it.

- Mark out and prepare the sides of the base of the ditch for the bottom layer of the retaining wall. Setting the timbers in gravel will make the job easier.

- Set the bottom layer of both sides of the revetting in place. Stretch a mason's

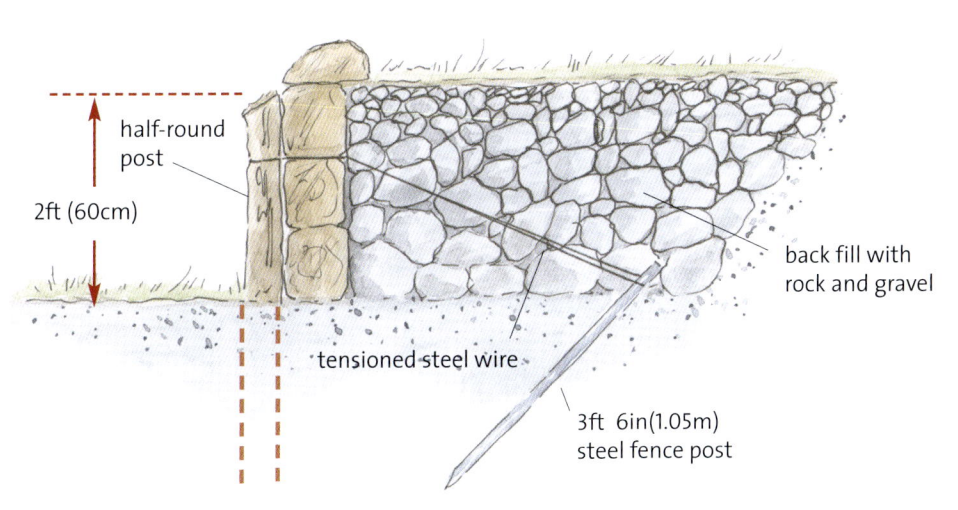

Side view of ditch showing how the revetting is anchored to a stake and back-filled with rock and gravel.

DESIGN AND BUILD A **CROSS-COUNTRY COURSE**

Curved open ditch under construction. Curved fences offer riders a choice of routes.

line tight along the length of the base layer. This ensures that it is straight. A 4ft (1.2m) level will help to keep both sides of the revetting at the same height. It is easier to build true to the bubble in the level. However, if the ditch naturally slopes downhill, then it makes sense to go with the ground.

- Toe-nail the joins using 8in (20cm) nails. This will keep the wall rigid during construction.

- Build the wall of railway sleepers (ties) until the top sleeper is level with the ground. Toe-nail the joins as you build. It is better to have the sides leaning out 5° to offset all the forces pushing the revetting in.

- Half-round posts are used on the inside of the ditch. These are necessary at every join, or if 16ft (4.8m) timbers are used, then a post at every 8ft (2.4m). The half-rounds will only need to be dug in 12in (30cm) unless the ground is soft.

- Opposite each post dig a trench 3ft (90cm) back into the bank. These are for the retaining wire and anchor post.

- Take a 7ft (2.1m) steel fence post and cut it in half. A half piece of steel post or 'T' bar will be the anchor post. The simplest way of cutting a steel post is to cut it half way through with a hacksaw and then smack it with a sledge hammer.

- Pound the 'T' bars in at an angle approximately 3ft (90cm) in from the wall of railway sleepers (ties). A 10lb (5kg) sledge hammer gives you authority over obstructions.

- Nine or ten gauge mild steel galvanised is used to wire the half-round to the anchor post. Tie one end of the wire to the 'T' bar, using the hole in the bar. Pass it under the top railway tie, around the half-round, pull it tight and fasten it to the 'T' bar. Now take a 10in (25cm) nail, or something similar, and twist the wire to tighten it. By tensioning the wire the retaining wall is securely anchored to the 'T' bar. Repeat this procedure for the remaining posts.

- It is essential that the material used for backfilling will not subside or give way. Rocks and coarse gravel are best. The rocks should come up to within 6in (15cm) of the top. The remainder is filled with gravel – 0–¾in (0–20mm) crushed stone packs the best, but the sharp edges of the stones in this kind of gravel are a concern. A top dressing of screenings or stone-dust alleviates this problem. Pit-run gravel with its rounded stones is less harmful. The gravel can be packed by driving on it with a tractor. The footing will need to be checked regularly, as it will settle over time.

- A half-round nailed onto the top of the revetting will make the ditch easier for a galloping horse to see.

## SIMPLER CONSTRUCTION METHOD

- This method can be used when the ditch will never have running water in it. Instead of tying the revetting back, this method uses 16ft (4.8m) logs with brace logs jammed in either end to keep the two walls in position. These ditches are generally for the lower levels and consequently smaller and slightly shallower. Two logs deep will usually suffice. To keep everything in place, toe-nail the joins with 8in (20cm) nails. Telegraph poles that are suspected of having hidden nails buried in them are perfect candidates for this job.

- Excavate the ditch. The depth is between 18in (45cm) and 2ft (60cm); the width 2ft (60cm) wider than the finished jump.

- Place the two largest logs in the ditch. Check that they are level.

DESIGN AND BUILD A **CROSS-COUNTRY COURSE**

Revetted dry ditch (simple version).

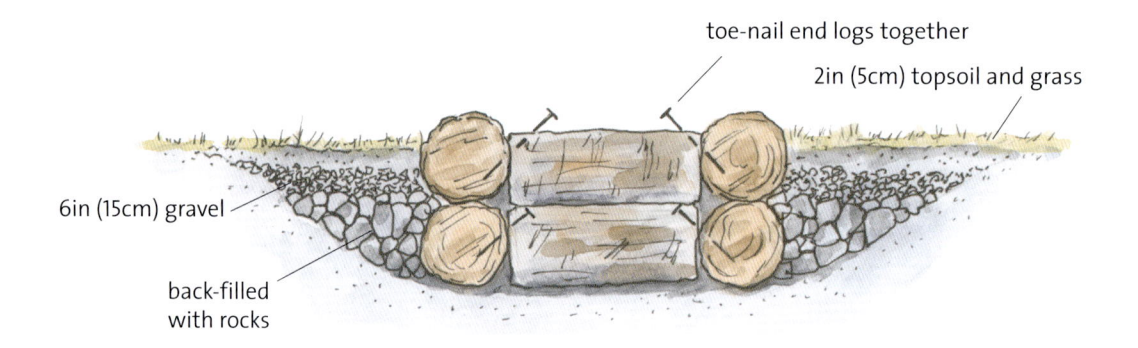

toe-nail end logs together

2in (5cm) topsoil and grass

6in (15cm) gravel

back-filled with rocks

- Wedge a short log at either end. These keep the main logs apart.
- Toe-nail the joins using 8in (20cm) nails.
- Place the second set of logs on top of the first.
- Wedge in the end logs and nail.
- Thoroughly pack rocks and gravel behind the logs.
- Cover the gravel with 2in (5cm) of topsoil and tamp it.

CHAPTER 8 | **MAINSTAY FENCES**

Trakehner (front view).
*(Photo: Charlotte Harper)*

## Trakehner

A trakehner is a big log suspended over a ditch. The size of the ditch and the airy gap between the log and the ditch are all part of the test. This is one of those fences where what a galloping horse sees, and what the spectators see from the side view, are very different. A well-built trakehner may look intimidating, but to a horse it is just another big log. The challenge for the builder is to reconcile the need for a huge log and the need to be able to dismantle the jump quickly and safely. A substantial ground-line log is necessary and this helps to reduce the airy look these fences tend to have. When viewed from a distance the jump looks like two big ascending logs. For the lower levels, a log over a ditch is a good introduction to trakehners. This is an easier fence to ride than an open ditch.

### MATERIALS

The same materials for a ditch plus :

1 log @ 16ft–18ft (4.8m–5.4m) long and 16in (40cm) diameter (top log)

1 log @ 16ft–18ft (4.8m–5.4m) long and 12in (30cm) diameter (ground-line)

DESIGN AND BUILD A **CROSS-COUNTRY COURSE**

Side view of trakehner, showing construction details.

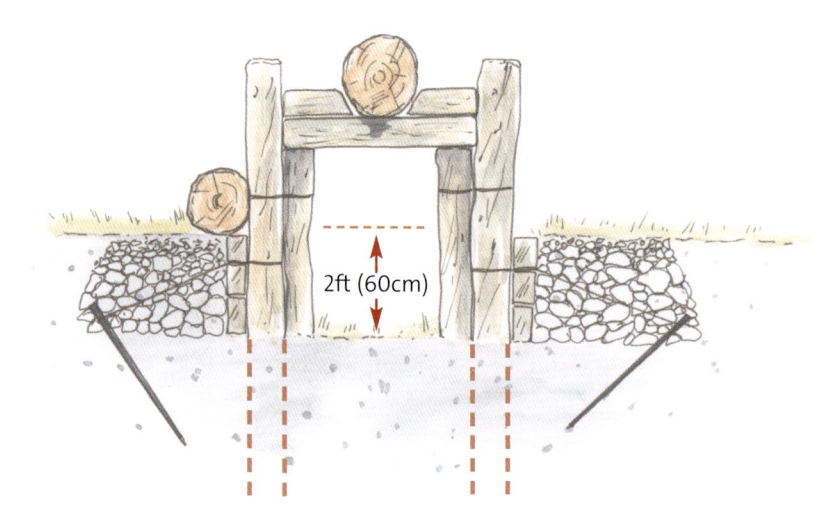

> 8 posts @ 8ft (2.4m) long and 10in (25cm) diameter (posts and frame to support top log)
>
> 25ft (7.5m) of 9-gauge mild steel wire and handful of 1½in (35mm) staples
>
> 6ft (1.8m) of nylon rope

## CONSTRUCTION METHOD

- Excavate and revett the ditch. As a rule of thumb, the ditch for a trakehner will be 12in (30cm) wider than an open ditch for a coffin.

- Set an 8ft (2.4m) post at each of the four corners of the ditch. These are on the outside of the retaining wall and if wired back to an anchor post will serve to retain the ends of the revetting timbers.

- The frame is built so that the top of the log will be 6in (15cm) below the maximum top height for the level of competition. Support posts are wired to the posts in the ground and a cross-member rests on these supports. Each cross-member is held in place by fitting it tightly between the posts.

- The log is then placed onto the cross-members.

- It is a judgement call whether the log is centred over the ditch, angled or positioned toward the back of the fence. The log must be securely locked in position. Wedging chocks between the log and the frame can do this. It is also roped to the frame.

- A substantial ground rail is roped to the front of the fence. This rail should be approximately 12in (30cm) in diameter. Having a good eye for a fence really helps in getting the proportions right for this type of fence.

> **TIPS**
>
> - It is unnecessary for the ditch to be more than 2ft (60cm) deep.
>
> - The height of the log is a judgement call. Generally 6in (15cm) below the maximum top height for that level of competition will be close to the mark.
>
> - There is an alternative construction method that has the support posts attached to the side of the posts. This method could be considered for the higher levels where the risks are greater, but my experience has been that if everything is built in proportion, then these fences ride well.
>
> - The gravel on both sides of the ditch should have a light sprinkling of topsoil and grass cuttings so that it blends in with the surrounding ground. The appearance of bright new gravel in front of the fence is a potential hazard as it may cause the horse to check slightly instead of maintaining balanced forward momentum.

## Drops

Riding over undulating terrain defines cross-country competitions and, to a large extent, the terrain determines whether a jump is a novice or an advanced question. Drops are a tempting way to upgrade a course but it is easy to overdo it. There are only so many competitions in a horse at the upper levels and these types of fence can take their toll on suspensory ligaments. The trick is to make the drop appear, to horse and rider, to be worse than it is. This is done by siting the jump just back from the edge of the slope and by the horse landing on a down slope rather than on level ground. For example, to have a 6ft (1.8m) drop off a bank built on the flat, build a ramp on the landing and raise the height of

# DESIGN AND BUILD A CROSS-COUNTRY COURSE

Above: Drop into woods. Above right: side view of drop prior to back-filling.

the log jump off the bank a corresponding amount. Drops into water pose a problem: too often the murky water hides a steep drop onto a hard level surface. Although the water may only be 9in (23cm) deep, it is still possible to provide a ramped landing that is just underwater.

There are many different types of fence that lend themselves to being drop jumps. They all have two things in common: they are not trappy, and are some form of ascending vertical without a significant top spread. At the lower levels a solid ascending ramp or ski jump works well. A more challenging question is a chevron jump on a down slope and the first element of a coffin combination. The chevron was used as a symbol in prehistory to represent the ocean wave and as a metaphor for life, being both everlasting and having sudden surprises. However, I suspect riders don't always pick up on the subtle messages in the course design.

# 9.

# Combinations

THE SECRET TO BUILDING A COMBINATION that rides well is to decide on the best line to ride it before it is built. Marking out the proposed combination with stakes and rope and then visualising the fence from fifty yards/metres away to get an accurate assessment, is time well spent. There is always an optimum site for every jump and for the more complicated ones it is a good practice not to rush into the construction. It is well worth the effort to stake it out and then have a critical look at it the next morning.

At the lower levels of competition the combinations are little more than a gymnastic exercise with one or two strides between the elements. These have their place, but I prefer to have more emphasis on educating and testing the riders rather than the horses. Having fences on a slight bending line will do this. If the horse is not properly presented to the fence in the correct frame then the competitor risks a run-out. These kinds of combinations are quick and simple to put together, especially if the second element is a portable fence. Elaborate combinations that have many alternative routes are magnificent in a Balaclava kind of way and may even be justified as prestige expense. But generally the same question can be asked by adapting the design to fit the terrain. The money saved can then be directed where it is most needed – footing, facilities and prize money.

When setting out to design combinations, walk the land and work with the natural features and the terrain. The goal is to have the combination fit so naturally into the landscape that it looks as though it has always been there. To do this is actually easier than it sounds. The metaphor of a jigsaw puzzle has been used to describe the process of course design, and it is very apt. The trick is to let your intuition guide you, rather than trying to force the pieces together. I start by building the jumps that are obvious, what they are and where they go. While I am working on those ones, my subconscious is working on designing the remainder of the course. This process works best when you are on your own and undisturbed.

The first step in designing combinations is to know the questions you want to ask and where on the course it is appropriate to ask them. By the third fence horses should be firing on all cylinders. A pair of ascending rails positioned at right angles, or a similar type of turning question, demands control and lets horses know they've got a job to do and need to listen to the pilot. Similarly a ditch with a log over it, followed by a fence at a related distance, will prepare competitors for a coffin combination later on the course. The first complex should inspire confidence and result in horse and rider working in unison. This will help them negotiate the more challenging fences without having a difference of opinion.

Overconfidence, falling asleep at the wheel and bringing along a young horse too quickly, are all faults that the design should discourage. There are riders in every competition who are the weakest link and need to find a coach or go back and do their homework. Here are two examples of designs that can result in run-outs for the subway riders. The first is an unassuming jump on a bending line a few strides before a water jump, and the second is a three-element combination with the final fence on a bending line. Both questions are straightforward, so long as the rider remembers that water jumps are distracting and that the approach is critical for fences on a bending line. The designer's aim is not to trick riders or even to sort out competitors aggressively, but rather to address the problem of how safe jumps can become hazardous if not ridden to the standard expected at that level of competition. Combinations should tickle the riders so that they are wide-awake and focused.

There are many different types of combinations. Some are almost mandatory for every competition, but others will depend upon the terrain and their appropriateness for that level of competition. It is important that there is a natural progression of challenge. One particular fence or combination will serve to set horses up for the next one. For example, a trakehner would come after a coffin, and a steeplechase before a ditch and brush. This does not mean that a course gets progressively more difficult. But rather, by the judicious use

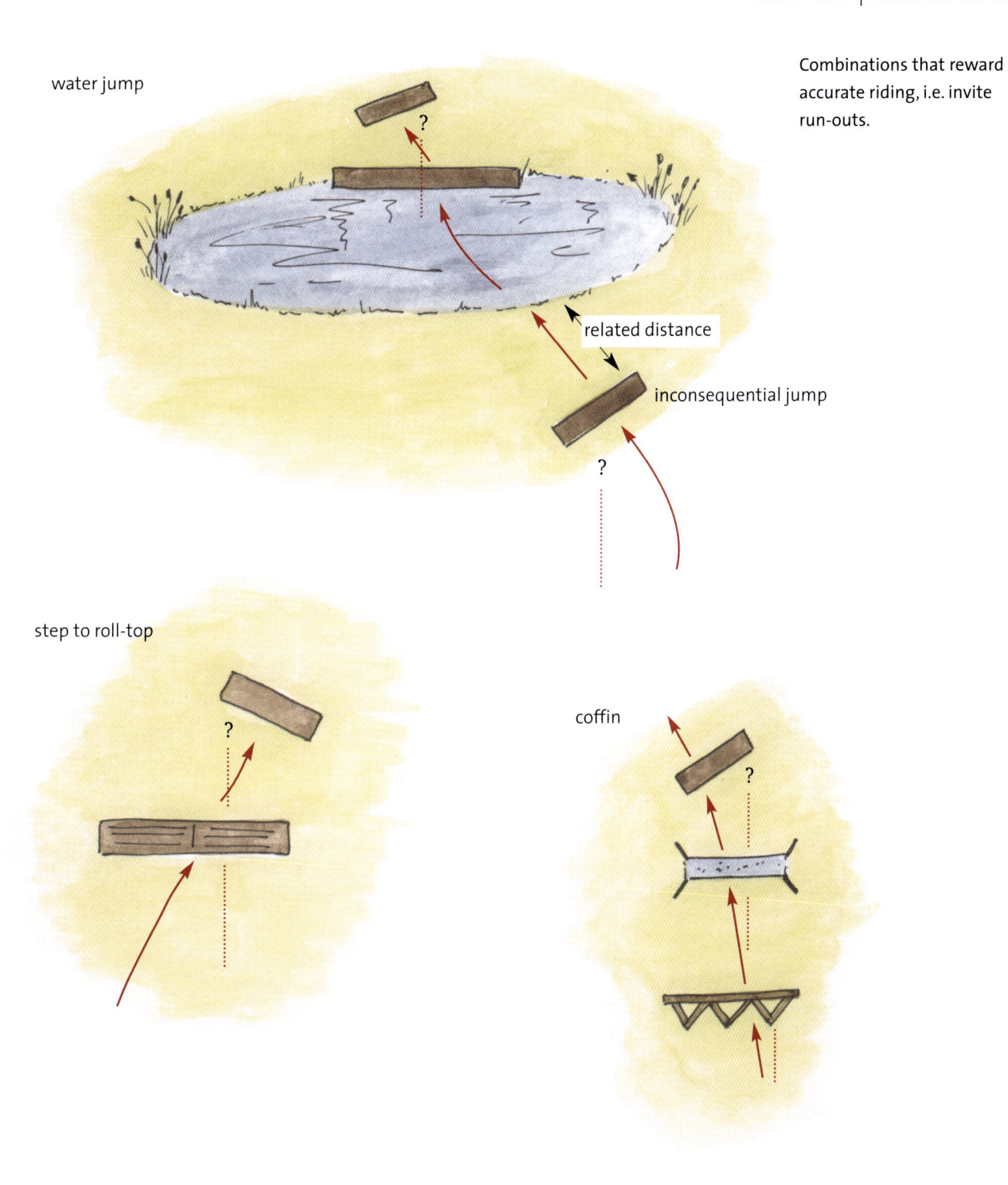

CHAPTER 9 | **COMBINATIONS**

Combinations that reward accurate riding, i.e. invite run-outs.

water jump

related distance

inconsequential jump

step to roll-top

coffin

97

of confidence-inspiring filler fences and well-thought-out combinations, the course will be a seamless display of balanced and controlled riding. When considering whether or not a fence is appropriate, I like to ask myself – 'Would my mother pop over this fence hacking to the meet on her young horse, or would she have to bang sparks off her spurs and have hounds roaring in front of her?'

## Different types of combination

Designing and siting combinations is one of the designer's more challenging tasks, and even at the best of times the results are often the scene of vigorous debate. For this reason some upper level combinations, bounces in particular, have not been included here, as they require more than a few notes in a book to lay out successfully. It is also a balancing act between having the appropriate level of difficulty and introducing easier examples of combinations that belong in the next level of competition. For example: a turning question combination can work for the lower levels by increasing the number of strides and widening the angles between the elements. Then there are other tests, such as hillside rails, that really only belong at the upper levels.

There are many different kinds of combination. Here is a brief description of eight of the most useful ones: farm pen, road crossing, sunken road, coffin, hillside rails, quarry in and out, double corners and offset rails.

### Farm pen

This is one of the simplest of all combinations. A well-tried format consists of a set of ascending rails with one or two strides to a spread fence, such as a farm shelter or cabin. There are many design possibilities offering different options and routes for several levels of competition. It is an admirable goal that combinations have a theme and reflect the heritage of the region – nevertheless jumps must be built with the horse rather than the spectator in mind. Vertical gates belong in that unfortunate category of potentially dodgy jumps that may ride successfully some of the time. For the lower levels of competition, big ascending logs are a better choice.

CHAPTER 9 | **COMBINATIONS**

Farm pen

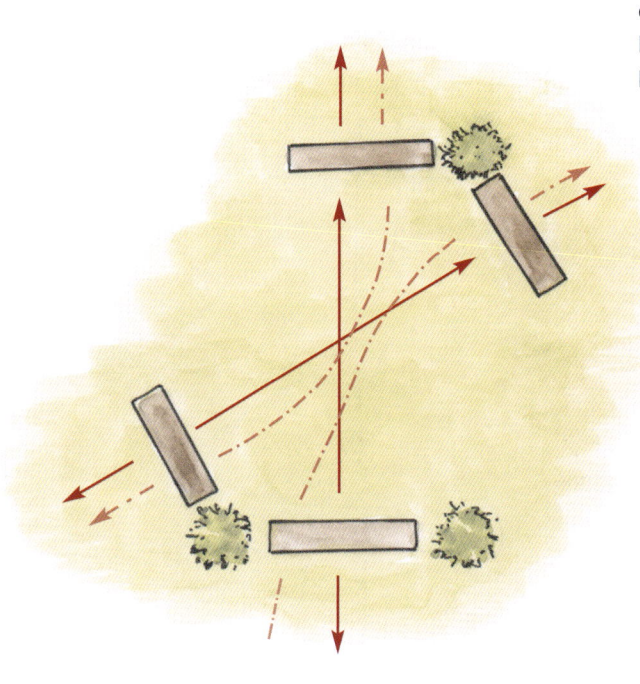

cabin

flower bed

hog's back

stone wall

Multiple-use farm-pen combination for the lower levels. Distance on bending line at least three strides.

99

Road crossing.

cordwood

ascending logs

## Road crossing

A pair of fence lines frames the jumps in this type of combination. Generally the distance between elements is at least two or three strides. These attributes combine to make for a very inviting fence and consequently the dimension of both elements can be close to maximum. Ascending logs to a cordwood is one suggestion for this kind of site. The roadway between the fences has to be made safe. Is the surface too hard, uneven, slippery or creating an illusion? These problems all have to be rectified and are discussed in the chapter on footing. Jumping from light to dark and from dark to light may also be a factor. In this situation the jumps should be stained or built so that they are easily assessed by a galloping horse.

## Sunken road

Sunken roads are to course builders what sunken ships are to treasure hunters. Many a lost afternoon have I spent crawling under briars hoping to come across the remains of a long forgotten roadway. When cleaned up and polished these sites are a wonderful opportunity to be original and creative: the challenge can

CHAPTER 9 | **COMBINATIONS**

Left: Sunken road. Above: Second element of sunken road. *(Photos: Charlotte Harper)*

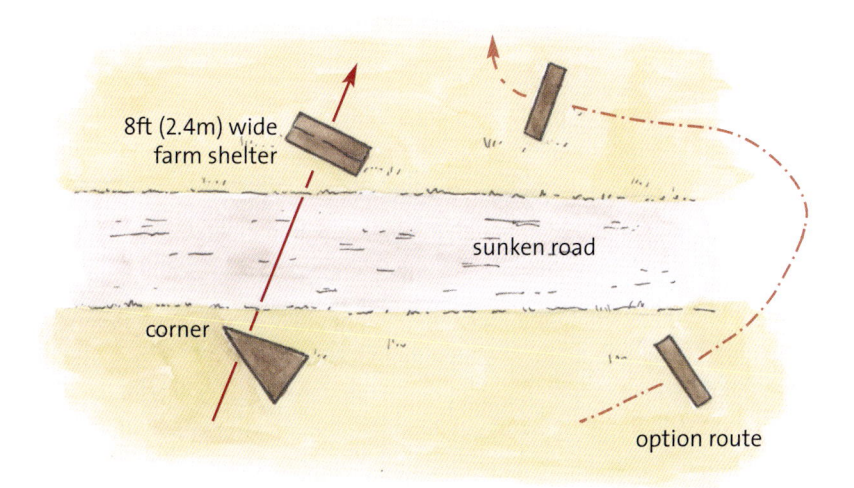

8ft (2.4m) wide farm shelter

sunken road

corner

option route

The striding through a sunken road is critical regardless of whether the slopes are left natural or revetted.

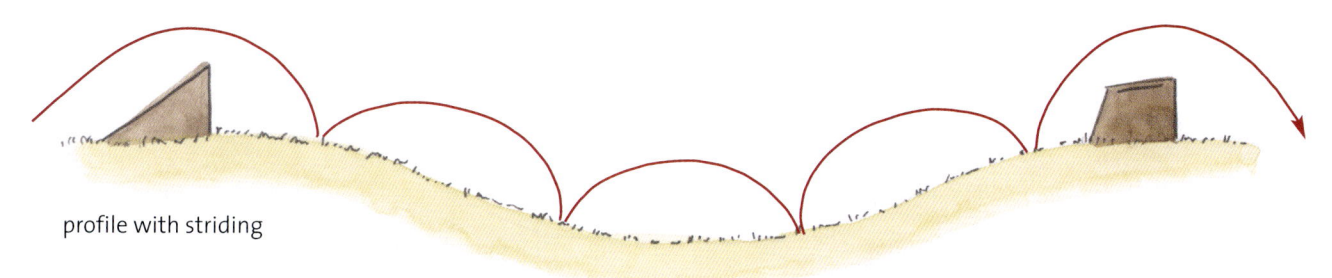

profile with striding

101

# DESIGN AND BUILD A CROSS-COUNTRY COURSE

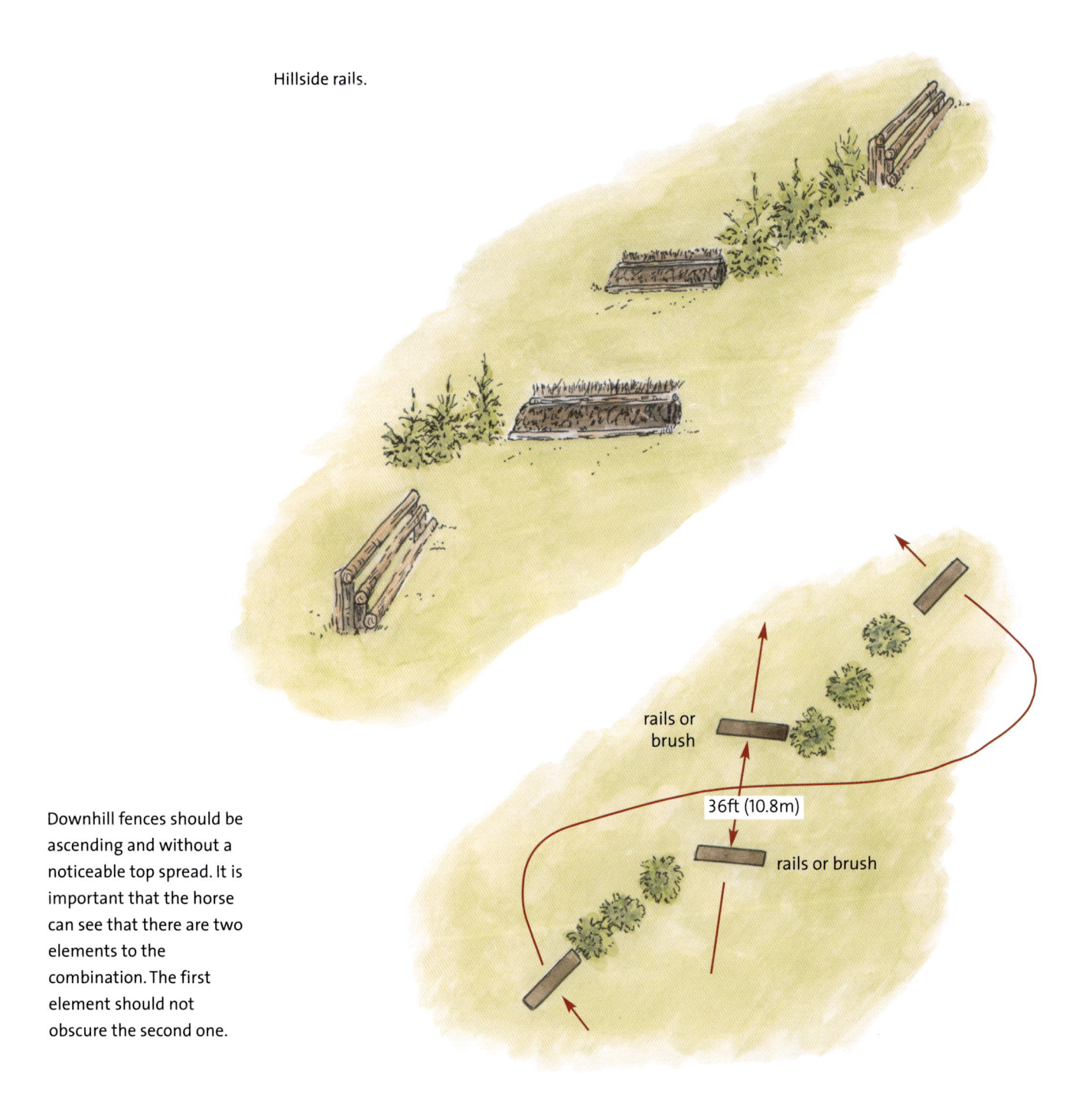

Hillside rails.

rails or brush

36ft (10.8m)

rails or brush

Downhill fences should be ascending and without a noticeable top spread. It is important that the horse can see that there are two elements to the combination. The first element should not obscure the second one.

102

be ratcheted up a notch and alternative routes designed that make sense. In its simplest form a sunken road consists of jumps on the higher ground on either side of a road. The designer sets the striding for controlled and balanced riding. The hardcore will want to blast through a sunken road like an express train through a commuter station. They might consider taking a pull if the fences are corners and skinnies rather than generous logs. The alternative route should not be an afterthought, but rather ask an easier, similar question that takes longer to answer. The slow routes work best when they create displays of seamless riding, rather than make the rider look like a wind-surfer. If the sides of the sunken road are weak they may have to be revetted. The disadvantages to this are that it doubles the number of jumping efforts, locks the horse into a set distance and turns the combination into a grid. This is fine for young horses. But it is better for competitions if riders have to hold a line and present their horse properly to the fence. It is critical that the striding is correct when fences are positioned close to the sloped slides of a sunken road.

## Hillside rails

This type of downhill combination should be carefully thought out. Hillside rails are a good test when well sited, but they can also easily submerge into the swamp of failed experiments. The problem they pose to designers is how to minimise the chance of them being attacked with a horse too much on the forehand. Siting the rails off a sweeping turn helps to alleviate this possibility. This combination consists of a pair of curved ascending rails or brush: the first element is generally concave and the second one is convex. The two elements are sited so that the optimum route presents the rider with jumps that have a narrow face. The advantage of using brush is that the fence is both more imposing and more forgiving.

## Quarry combinations

When a sponsor comes running up to you with wads of cash, a quarry combination becomes a possibility. Take a piece of sloped ground and excavate a horseshoe-shaped cut into the slope. Then build a field-stone retaining wall around the edge. The wall is capped with timber. There are various refinements and possibilities for alternatives and routes for different levels of competition. One end of it could be a freestanding stone wall, jumpable from either direction.

# DESIGN AND BUILD A **CROSS-COUNTRY COURSE**

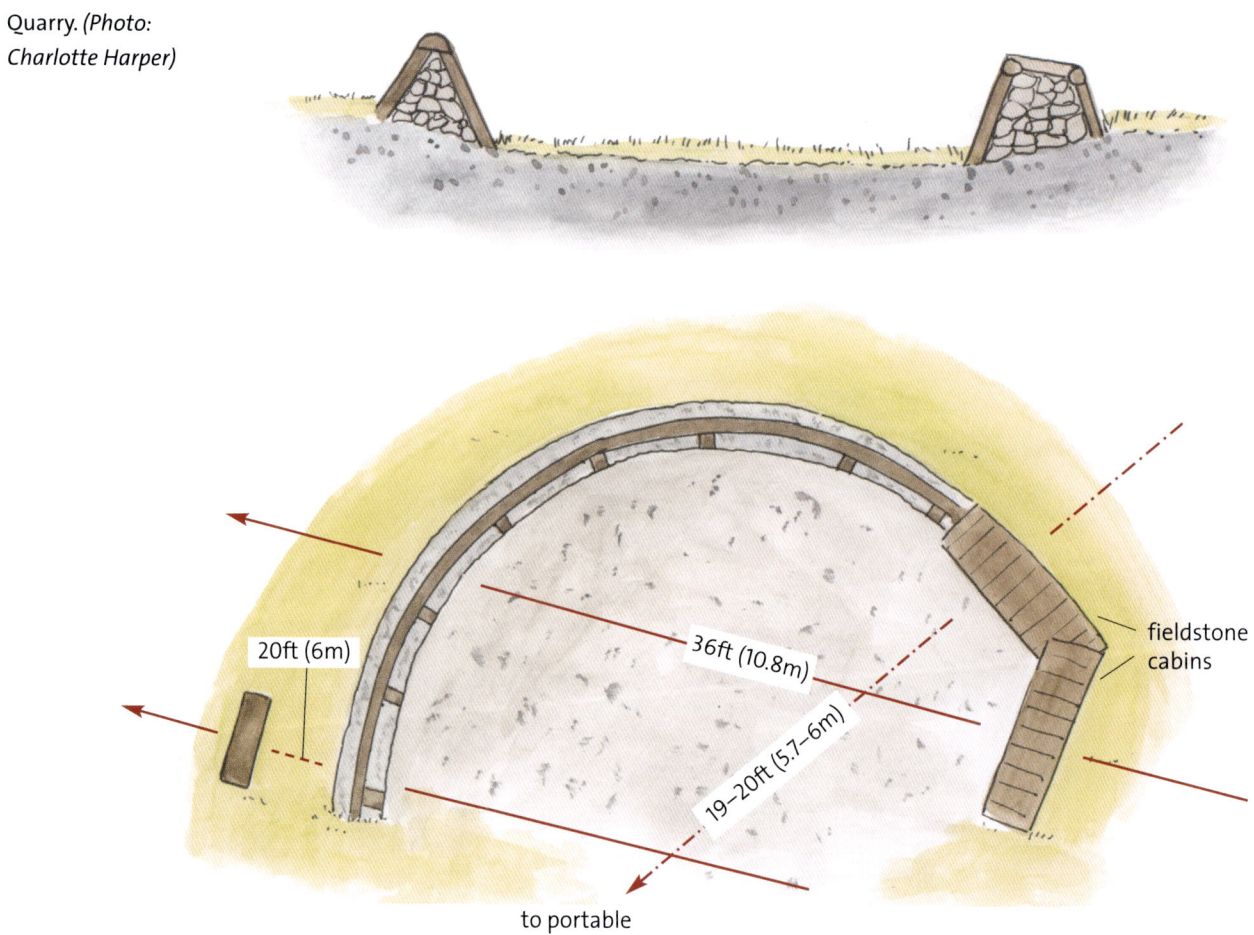

Quarry. *(Photo: Charlotte Harper)*

20ft (6m)

36ft (10.8m)

19–20ft (5.7–6m)

fieldstone cabins

to portable

104

CHAPTER 9 | **COMBINATIONS**

Portable fences can be strategically placed in or around the outside perimeter. These are good-looking complexes and very useful with all their options. But they are expensive and time-consuming to build.

## Double corners

The day may come when the wobblers find out that the challenge of jumping corners is all in the head. In the meantime coaches do very nicely from these fences. For the designer they ask all the right questions of horsemanship with only a modest cost in materials and labour. If the first corner is very slightly offset in relation to the second one, then it can be jumped on its own. This allows for two levels of competition to make use of the same combination. The first corner is built to maximum dimensions for the lower level of competition and they will jump only this one. The upper level of competition will jump both corners. Two strides (34ft–36ft/10.2m–10.8m) between the corners works well. Keep in mind that striding distances should be a fraction shorter when more accurate riding is demanded. It does take a certain amount of skill in getting the positioning of the corners exactly right. The options to the corners can also be interchangeable between the different levels of competition. It is critical that the striding is exact and the approach is clear and free of distractions. A wavering

top of both corners is planked

Double corner.

105

DESIGN AND BUILD A **CROSS-COUNTRY COURSE**

Bird's eye view of double corners.

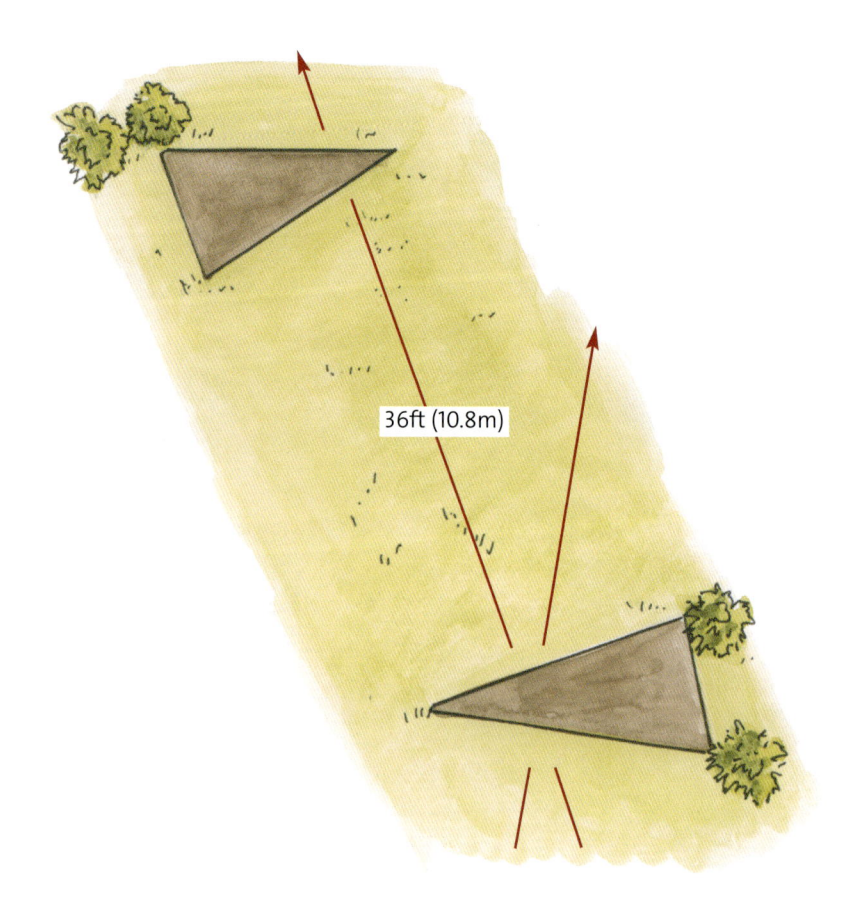

36ft (10.8m)

horse should have a run-out rather than an attempt at the widest part of the corner. Blocking off the unjumpable section with substantial evergreens prevents this. Planking the top makes corners safer and, if warranted, the sides could also be planked.

## Offset rails

It is the day before the competition, there are still two combinations to build and the lumber pile is down to three logs and a handful of posts. The answer is an offset rail combination that has one route for novice (preliminary) and another for intermediate. Both levels ride the first element. The second element is a log set at just under right angles to the first element. The upper-level second element is to the left and the lower level one is to the right. Both elements have to be ridden at an angle and there is a route between them that is exactly one

CHAPTER 9 | **COMBINATIONS**

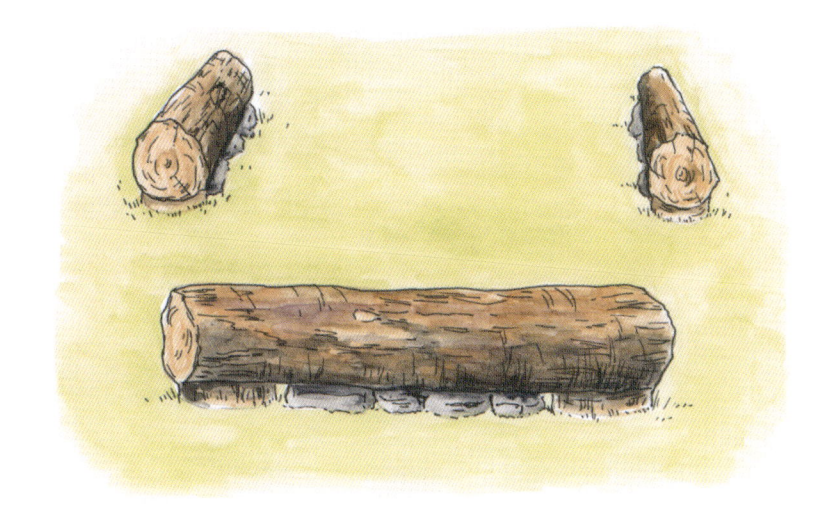

Offset logs.

Bird's-eye view showing optimum lines and alternative route.

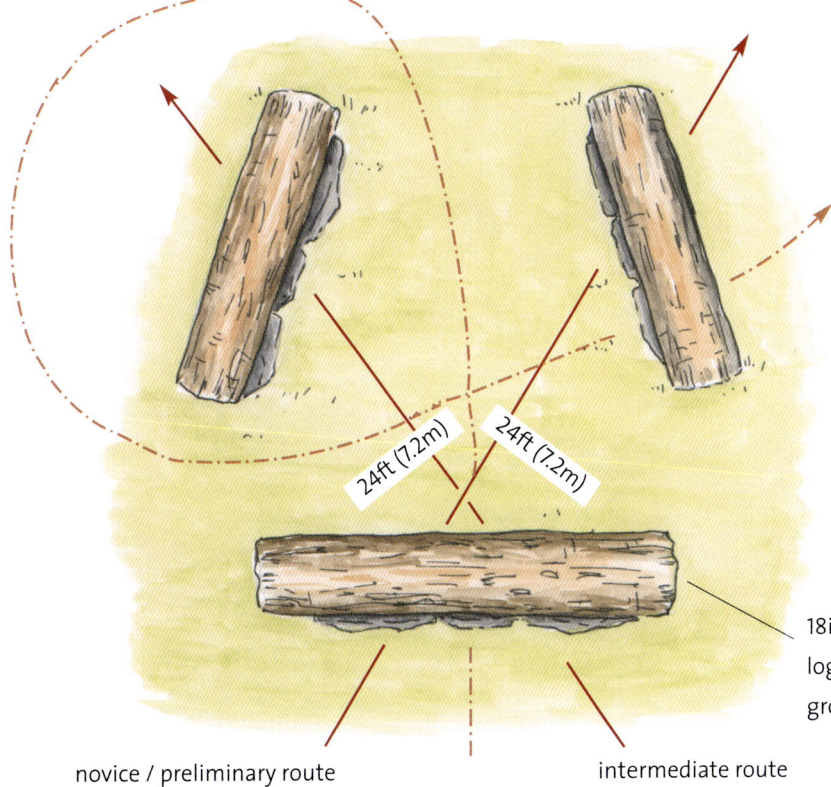

option route

24ft (7.2m)

24ft (7.2m)

18in–24in (45cm–60cm) log with boulders for groundline

novice / preliminary route

intermediate route

107

# DESIGN AND BUILD A **CROSS-COUNTRY COURSE**

*Offset cordwoods. (Photo: Claus Zander)*

stride (24ft/7.2m). The gaps between the jumps are wide enough so that a horse can run out. Construction is simple: the logs should be at least 18in–24in (45cm–60cm) in diameter and are supported by posts. Two or three big boulders are dragged into position under each log, and they are the ground-line. A call to the local garden centre might result in the loan of potted shrubs and a gnome or two. These decorate the fence and fill in any gaps in the ground-line. It is flagged as an AB combination for intermediate, and as two separate fences for novice (if you are kind). The gaps between the jumps are wide enough so that the slow route is over the first element, through the gap and circle to the second element.

## Coffins

A coffin is one of the most useful and versatile of all combinations and is an essential ingredient to any course. It is usually sited in a shallow dip in the land and comprises an open ditch sandwiched between a pair of rails. When designers nudge up the challenge they should also nudge up the jump's ridability. The following points will help horse and rider be successful:

- The approach must be conducive to balanced and controlled riding.

- The first element is generally an ascending post and rails, although at the

CHAPTER 9 | **COMBINATIONS**

Coffin. (The rails to the left of the ditch are just a wing.) *(Photo: Charlotte Harper)*

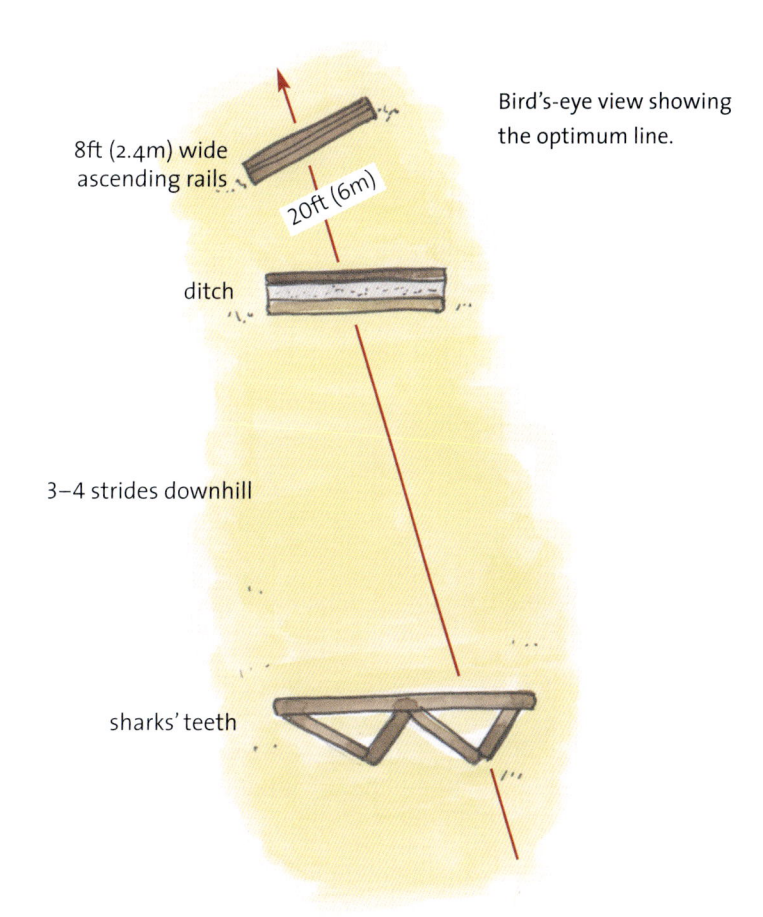

Bird's-eye view showing the optimum line.

8ft (2.4m) wide ascending rails

20ft (6m)

ditch

3–4 strides downhill

sharks' teeth

109

upper levels a sharks' teeth is more impressive. The main point is that the first element is appropriate for sloping terrain and does not obscure the remainder of the combination.

- The ditch must be clearly defined. It is recommended that a half-round be nailed to the top of the revetting on the take-off side. A log over the ditch makes it much easier for the lower levels.

- By siting the third element on a bending line, both the challenge and usefulness of the combination is increased (it can be jumped as a half-coffin by lower-level competitors).

The diagram is one example of a novice-level coffin. The distance between the centre of the ditch to the centre of the third element is exactly one stride: if a horse drifts out then a run-out is likely as he will meet the rails on an 'off' stride.

# 10.

# Banks and Steps

Banks and steps turn a collection of jumps into a cross-country course. They can be used on their own or as the nucleus of a combination. There are countless ways to use them to test competitors. There are also countless ways that they test the workmanship of course builders. These structures are expected to last for many years and must be hard-wearing. The key elements are striding, footing and revetting. Accessing the right distance for the striding is straightforward, as horses are in a frame and there are set distances that apply to the many different types of banks. The footing on a flat-top bank is strengthened by building it up in layers. The base should be rocks or other material that will remain solid, regardless of the weather, followed by a 6in (15cm) layer of gravel and capped with a few inches/cm top of screenings. There are tricks and techniques that will ensure that the retaining wall, or revetting as it is called, will withstand the dilapidations of time and skidding hooves.

## Banks

There are three main types of bank: the flat-topped Normandy bank, the rounded Irish bank, and the multi-tiered bank. The first consideration when building a bank is the amount of fill required. If there is a rock pile or mound of clay, it is a relatively simple job to shape and frame it up into a bank. For example, an old fence line can be cleared and the rocks and rubble can be pushed up to form the base of the bank. Three other considerations are land use, terrain and versatility. Because they are permanent structures, they should fit into the overall site plan. High ground makes them more imposing, more visible and less affected by wet weather. However, like water jumps, they should be versatile and ridable from as many directions as possible. This is a strong argument for building them out in the open, particularly if schooling is their primary function.

## Normandy bank

- Mark out the four corners. When the diagonals are the same length, the corners are square.

- A bounce bank is 10ft 6in–11ft (3.15m–3.3m) across the top.

- A one-stride bank is between 17ft 6in and 19ft 6in (5.25m and 5.85m).

- A two-stride bank is 28ft–30ft (8.4m–9m).

- Generally the design allows for at least two routes. For example, one route will be one stride, and the easier route two strides.

- Railway sleepers (ties), telegraph poles or pressure-treated lumber are the most commonly used construction materials. Set out the first layer. The sides must be straight and level. A mason's line, a line level and a 4ft (1.2m) level will keep the sides true.

- The ends of the timbers are toe-nailed together with two 6in or 8in (15cm or 20cm) nails. This helps hold the structure together during construction.

- The optimum height for the revetting is 2ft 9in (82.5cm). If the sides are too low then there is a possibility of a horse stumbling instead of jumping. Three-feet (90cm) high revetting is more suitable to the fitter and more athletic upper-level competitor. Keep in mind that the gravel will reduce the height by at least 3in (75mm). Build the wall, one layer at a time. It helps to have the wall lean slightly in toward the centre of the bank; this offsets some of the forces pushing it out. An outward leaning wall has a false ground-line and will need to be rebuilt.

- On the outside of the retaining wall, dig in a half-round post at every join or

CHAPTER 10 | **BANKS AND STEPS**

Normandy bank.

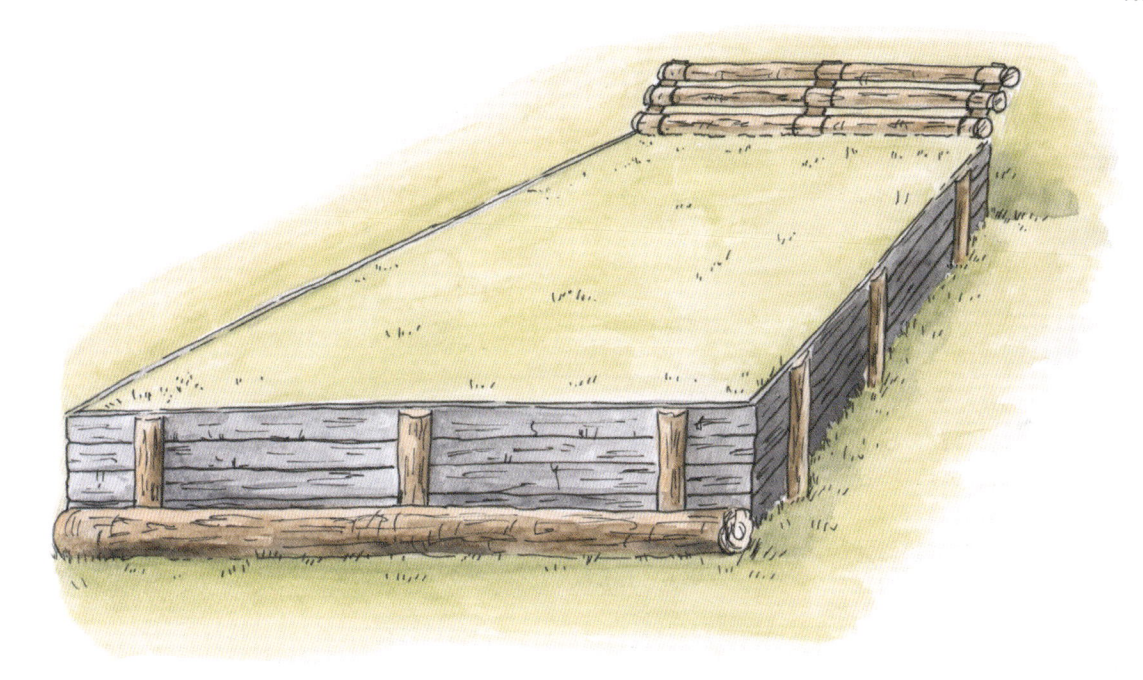

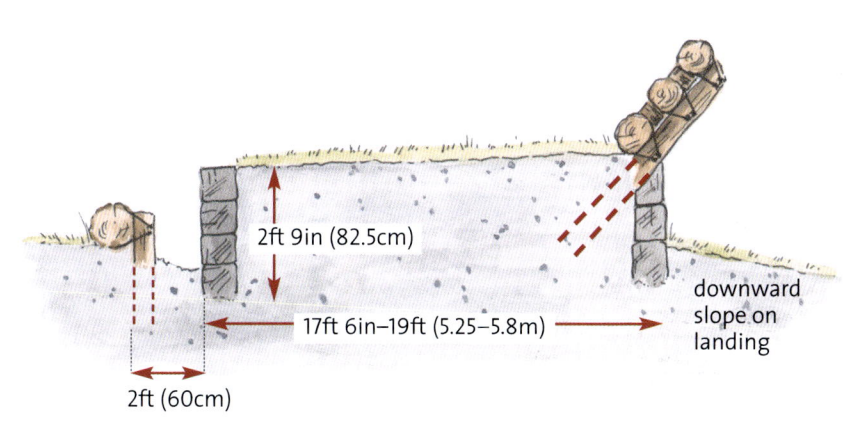

Profile of a one-stride Normandy bank. The striding distance on the bank will need to be adjusted to individual circumstances.

at every 8ft (2.4m). These posts are wired back to a 3ft (90cm) steel fence post that has been driven in on the inside of the wall opposite the post.

- Nine or ten gauge galvanised mild steel wire is fastened to the steel fence post, passed through the retaining wall between the top two layers of timbers, around the post and tied back to the anchor post. The wire is twisted tight, Spanish windlass style, using a long nail or rod.

113

DESIGN AND BUILD A **CROSS-COUNTRY COURSE**

- Rip-rap (5in–6in/12.5–15cm rocks) is the best choice to backfill behind the revetting. But any mix of rocks and coarse gravel that will provide a strong base and not subside can be used. It is not safe to use sand or topsoil to backfill immediately behind the revetting. Identifying and rectifying sub-standard revetting highlights what a thankless task technical delegates have. If you are working on an existing course and have doubts concerning the quality of the revetting, then it must be ripped out and rebuilt. It is too important a safety issue to give just a cursory inspection to existing structures.

- Many banks are built successfully using the fill from excavations. Allow several months for the clay to settle and a season for grass to become established. A short cut is to pack it with a bulldozer or drive on it with a tractor. Grass can be up in three weeks when raked into topsoil, covered in a light manure mulch and watered. During the excavation it is important to keep the topsoil separate from the clay subsoil. This is because soils high in organic matter, while good for top dressing, are often too friable to pack well.

- If there is going to be a jump off the bank, the posts should be positioned before the revetting is backfilled. The jump could be a log or rails, but there must be no gaps that a horse could drop a foot through. The height of the rails is a judgement call that is partially governed by the height of the drop. At the lower levels, the drop should be considerably less than it appears. The landing off a bank should always slope away so as to reduce jarring on horses' legs.

- It is a good idea for one of the sides to be a ramp rather than a wall. This allows a tractor to be used to pack the footing and adds to versatility.

- A bounce bank can be made to appear more challenging and at the same time safer by having a small ditch on the take-off side immediately in front of the revetting. It assists the horse in landing and taking off from the optimum point.

- Banks with one or more strides are built following the same directions. To assess the distance on a bank allow for a 10ft–11ft (3.3m–3.6m) stride and 3ft (0.9m) for both landing and take-off.

- It is critical that the backfilling behind the revetting is done with rocks and gravel. It must then be packed so that there is no chance of it giving way as a horse lands or takes off. The front tyres of a tractor are effective at compressing material. The edges have to be done by hand.

- It is best to have a gravel or screenings top dressing for the first year as this is when the most maintenance is expected. The following year grass should be encouraged by adding a small amount of topsoil and seeding. The grass stabilises the surface and is kinder to horses.

- A half-round nailed to the top layer of revetting will help define the jump for horses.

- A bank does not have to be revetted on all four sides. It is more useful at the lower levels to have a ramp on or off the bank and then have a fence two or three strides away on a bending line.

## Irish bank

These are great fun to ride, but to build them requires either deep pockets or a serious amount of fill that needs a home. The most important safety concern of this type of bank is that there is no possibility of a horse attempting to clear the bank in one huge bound. This is prevented by their height and the width across the top.

There are no hard and fast rules with the dimensions. Five feet (1.5m) high, 16ft –18ft (4.8m–5.4m) wide at the base and 10ft (3m) wide on top will work well. The bank should be 30ft–40ft (9m–12m) long, as this reduces the chance

Irish bank.

DESIGN AND BUILD A **CROSS-COUNTRY COURSE**

Irish bank in profile.

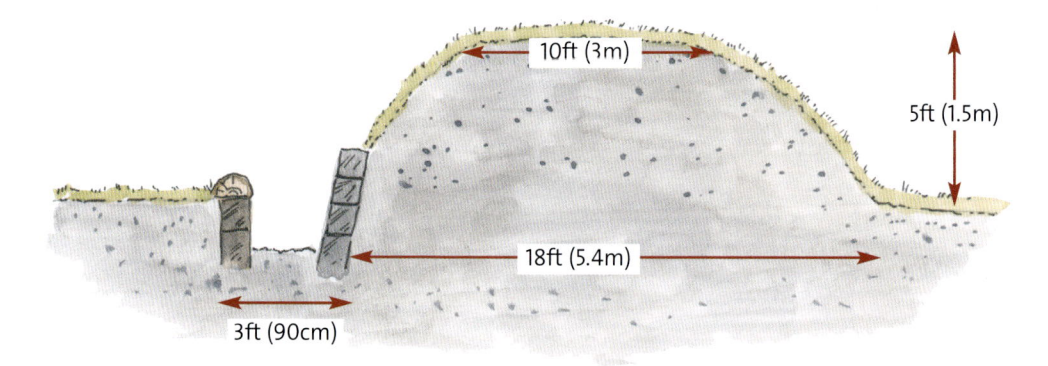

of horses tearing a hole in the side from all jumping in the same spot. The face of the bank is sloped so that horses are not asked to jump higher than the maximum top height for that level of competition. In practice a different section of the bank should be used each year so that the sod has time to recover.

The lower part of the sides can be revetted with timber or a low field-stone wall. This is extra work but it does protect and give shape to the sides. A ditch on either or both sides is also an option. The bank must be shaped so that horses can jump up on the side, rather than slither across the top.

The construction is straightforward. As much of the core as possible should be rock. This core is then covered in topsoil and shaped to the right dimensions. Grass seed is lightly raked into the topsoil and covered with a thin sprinkling of manure. The manure provides shade and retains the moisture, but if too thick it will prevent germination. Allow six months for the topsoil to firm up and a good root base to become established.

Profile showing how to tie back revetting when it is not possible to put a post in the ground.

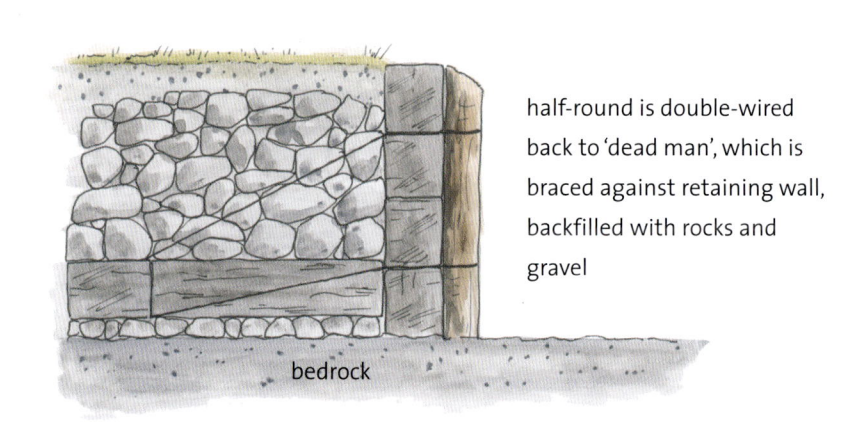

half-round is double-wired back to 'dead man', which is braced against retaining wall, backfilled with rocks and gravel

# CHAPTER 10 | BANKS AND STEPS

## Multi-tiered banks

These are the typical bank of three-day event courses. Their size, elaborateness or difficulty should not deter their construction on more modest courses or training centres. If there is enough fill available most of the work can be done by

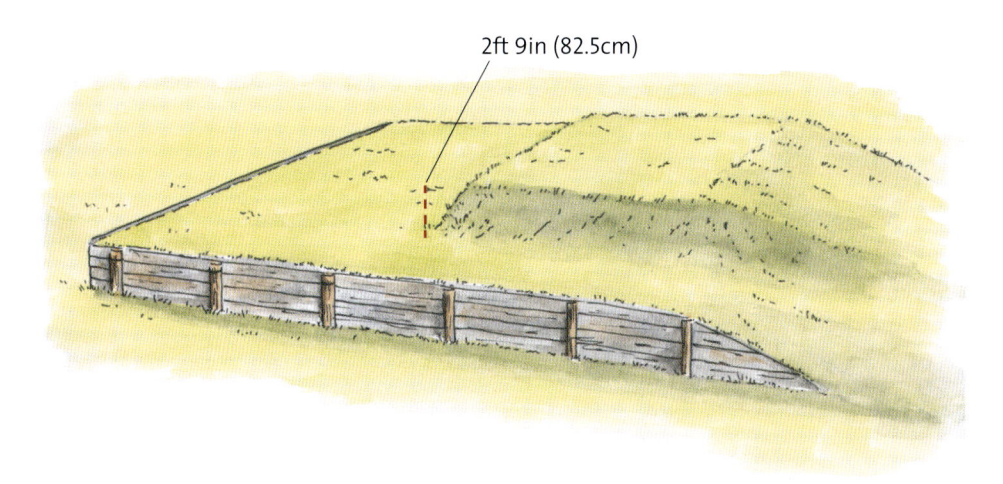

Two-tiered bank.

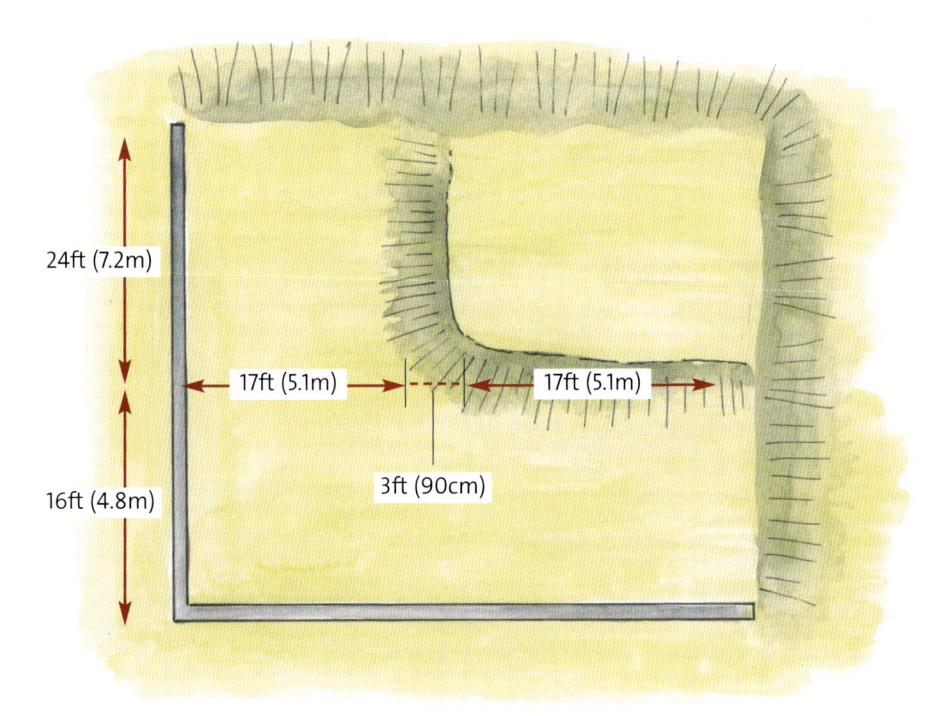

Bird's eye view of bank.

117

DESIGN AND BUILD A **CROSS-COUNTRY COURSE**

Multi-tiered bank.

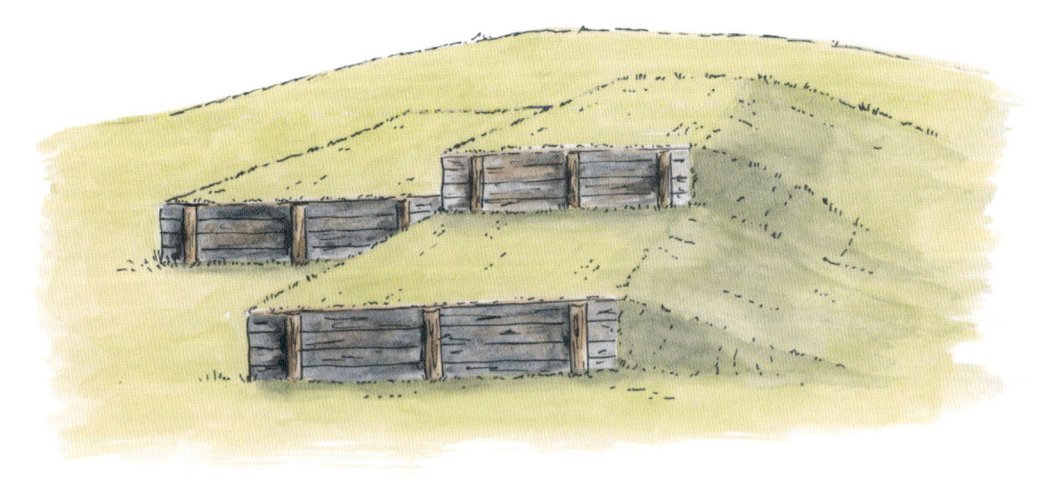

1 stride distance approx 17ft (5.1m); distances slightly shorter with multiple efforts

2ft 9in (82.5cm)

Bird's eye view of a two-tiered bank.

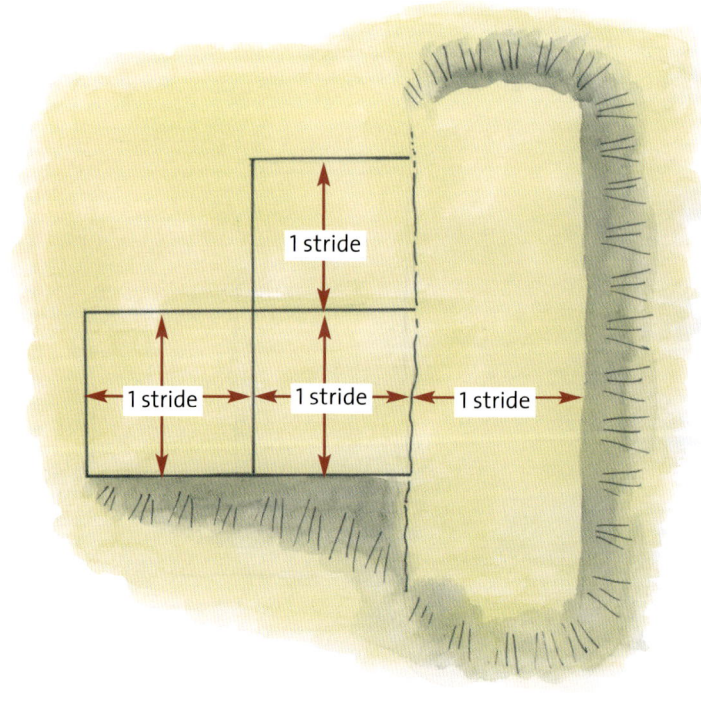

1 stride

1 stride | 1 stride | 1 stride

118

CHAPTER 10 | **BANKS AND STEPS**

Old three-sided bank.
*(Photo: Claus Zander)*

machine. The material excavated from a water jump is ideal for this kind of bank. However, it generally is too soft to be workable until it has had a few months to dry out. The location of a bank will depend upon local factors. But there are two points to keep in mind. If the bank is on high ground and dominates the sky line then it will look more impressive and be easier to sell to sponsors. If the budget does not allow for the fill to be trucked from the water jump, then build the bank nearby. It is a good principle of course design to lay out the track in swinging loops, not unlike a cloverleaf, so that the feature fences are in relative close proximity for the benefit of spectators and video coverage.

How ambitious the bank is will depend upon how much material is available and the level of competition. Here is a plan for a simple bank with two levels. The first layer is a 2ft 9in (82.5cm) high platform. Most of this will be revetted but it will need at least one ramped section so that a tractor can be driven onto the bank. The next level will be on the far left or right quadrant. It is easier to position jumps on the top of the bank if the far side of the bank slopes away at a 30° angle. It is not necessary to define the sides of each level with revetting. A steep grass-covered slope 2ft 9in (82.5cm) high allows for more flexibility in the striding.

As a rule of thumb, the landing and take-off points will be 3ft (0.9m) from the revetting and the stride will be in 10ft–11ft (3m–3.3m) increments. Regardless of the shape of the bank it is critical that the striding between the different levels be exact. The jump on the top of the bank should be uncomplicated. A large tree trunk or hanging log will work well in this situation.

# Steps

Steps are a very useful way of rewarding riders who ride with balance and control. A single step does not constitute a big athletic effort. But a fence a few strides after the step on a bending line is a safe way to penalise riders who are either asleep at the switch or out of control, by a run-out. Steps are straightforward to build. All that is required is to cut into a slope and revett the

Steps can either be cut into a slope or extend out from a slope as shown here.

2ft 9in (82.5cm)

joins toe-nailed together with 8in (200mm) nails

Side view of step.

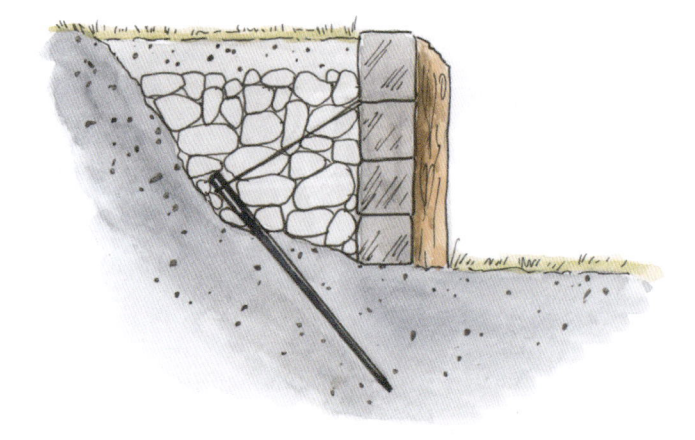

CHAPTER 10 | **BANKS AND STEPS**

Revetting that will become a step after right-hand side is backfilled with rock, gravel and topsoil.

sides. It is important not to over-face horses. At the lower levels a simple 2ft 9in (82.5cm) step is all that is required. From there you can go on to a pair of steps one or two strides apart. The fences immediately before or after the steps are generally more influential than the steps themselves.

- Before excavating it is necessary to mark out the steps with stakes. The grade also must be measured. If this is not done, then the slope before and after the step may be too steep. A hand-held sight level or a line level are both simple ways to measure the grade.

Step to hanging log.
*(Photo: Claus Zander)*

121

DESIGN AND BUILD A **CROSS-COUNTRY COURSE**

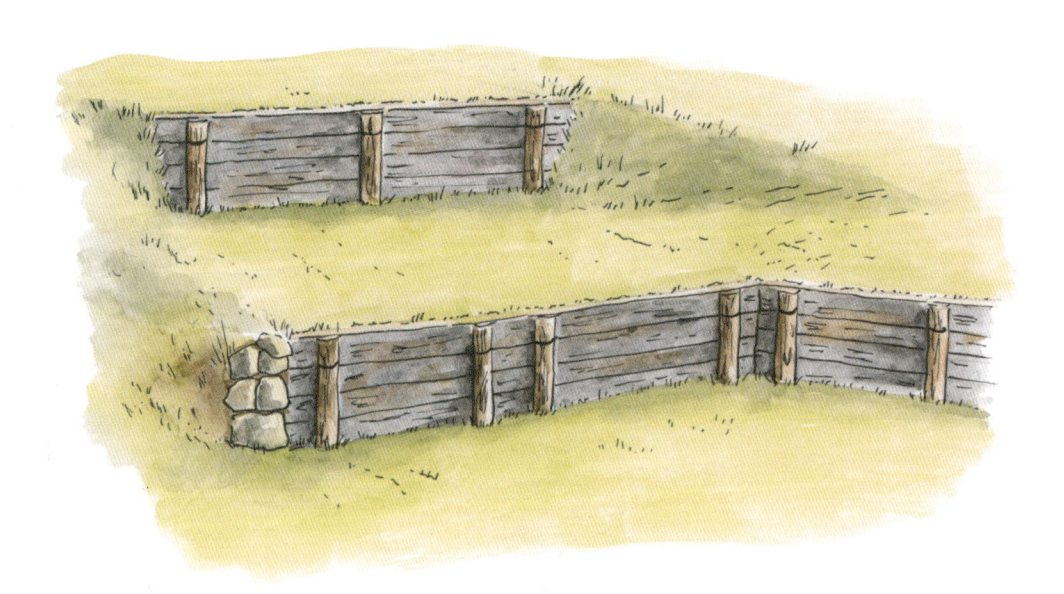

Two steps.

Side view of double steps.

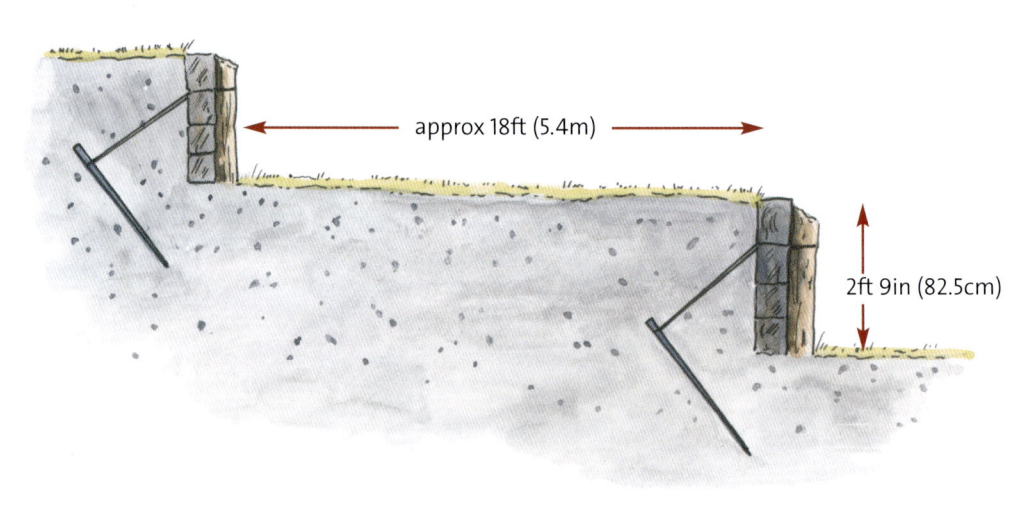

approx 18ft (5.4m)

2ft 9in (82.5cm)

5° from vertical

two steps    one step

122

CHAPTER 10 | **BANKS AND STEPS**

Triple steps.

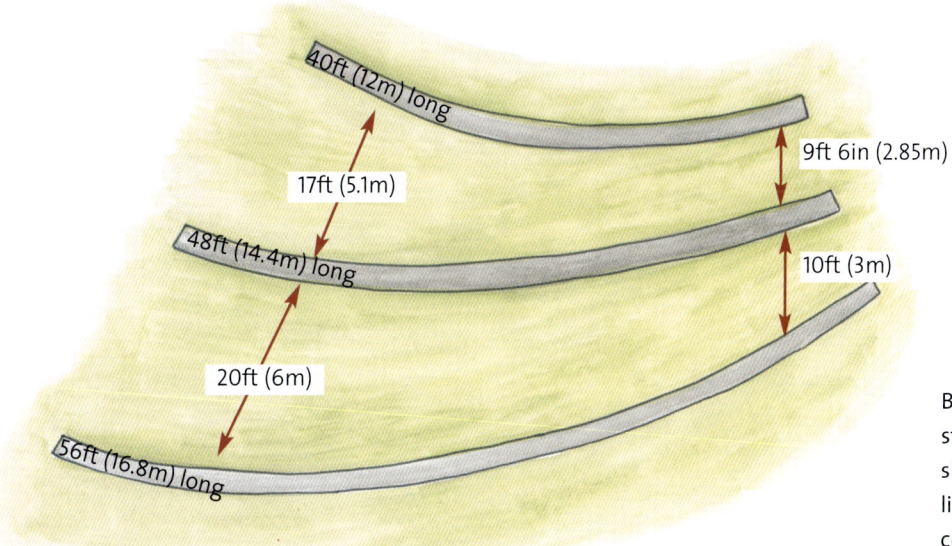

Bird's-eye view of triple steps. Note: the steps should be slightly curved like an eyelash, with the curve diminishing with each lower step.

- It is less work for the builder if the steps are excavated out of the hillside. But, if earth-moving equipment is not available, then you can build the steps on the side of the hill and backfill them with rocks.

- A series of three steps is common on upper-level courses. The striding distances are generally a foot shorter going downhill than going uphill. It is a

123

good idea to have the steps curved like an eyelash. This gives riders a choice of distances.

- When staking out the steps for the excavation, allow at least 2ft (60cm) for the revetting. Build the revetting 3ft (90cm) high, after the footing has been added the step will be 2ft 9in (82.5cm).

- If there are three steps, revett the centre one first. This is done because the excavation allows 2ft (60cm) for the revetting and if you start at the top or bottom step you could be out by the third step and have to dig into the bank.

- Whenever there are two or more steps it is useful if they are designed so that they can be jumped individually. This is done by having either curved steps or a section angled at one end. The complex can then be used by several levels of competition.

- Steps have the same revetting criteria as do banks and water jumps: the revetting must last for many years and it has to be tied back securely to an anchor post on the inside of the step.

- After the revetting is in place and has been backfilled with rock, then a top dressing of 4in (10cm) of screenings or 0–3/4in (0–20mm) gravel should be spread on the steps, particularly on the landing and take-off areas. It is best to have a gravel surface for the first year, and then add topsoil and seed. Good turf is the best material for stabilising a bank surface.

# 11.

# Water Jumps

Water complexes are the most exciting and challenging of all jumps to build. It is important to have a thorough understanding of all the variables as well as the design and construction process. There are four areas that you need to know about: choosing the best site, planning and design, construction, and fixing problems. The challenge and cost of building water jumps intimidates many people. It needn't be this way. The key point is always to work with nature; fighting nature empties your pocket and puts you on the losing side.

Where is the best location for the water jump? The plants answer this question. Cattails and bullrushes like standing water. A 3ft (0.9m) deep excavation in standing water will be a pond, not a water jump. Sedges and reeds grow in moist ground. This indicates that there is an impervious layer just beneath the surface – perfect for a water jump. Test holes will show the depth of the topsoil, the type of substrata and the likelihood of water. The next consideration is whether the gradient is suitable for a water jump.

If the proposed water jump is 50ft (15m) wide and there is a 3ft (0.9m) difference in the gradient, then after the excavation, one end will have a 6ft (1.8m) deep side. If the gradient is negligible, then the water jump will be difficult to drain if it becomes too full. Shooting sights with a transit makes an accurate picture of the grades. If a transit is not on hand, no problem. It is easy to make a simple device that will do the job. Rig up a 5ft (1.5m) pole with a short crosspiece at one end. The other end has a base so that it is free-standing, not unlike a sheet music stand. Place it in the middle of the proposed site. Mark the perimeter of the site with surveyors' stakes. Stand at each stake in turn; hold a 4ft (1.2m) level on your shoulder. Check that it is bubble level and look along the length of the level to the crosspiece in the centre of the site. Measure the distance from the top of the level to the ground. The difference in height between the crosspiece and the level is the difference in the grade. Use the information to draw a profile of the site. Move the stakes so that the proposed water jump will work with the gradient of the land.

The next step is the design, and this is decided by asking yourself, 'How can we have the most versatility at a reasonable cost?' Three strides by two strides, or approximately 50ft x 35ft (15m x 10.5m), is a practical size. The shape should be more rounded than square because corners become an unjumpable section. Maximum versatility within the constraints of budget and terrain are the criteria used to decide the design. An oval with alternating sections of revetting and ramps is one suggestion; the width of each route should be at least 16ft (4.8m) wide. The objective is to have as many routes and options as possible. (Revetting is the retaining wall that forms part of the side of the water jump.)

More test holes should be dug so that the design does not have to be changed during the excavation. The cost is calculated using the information gathered from the test holes. Several different designs for the site should now be drawn up and all will have a different price tag. For example: an island or promontory could be included in the design. In practice it is best to excavate a simple, rounded depression that requires the least amount of revetting, has good footing, the right amount of water and be within the budget.

The three principal costs are excavation equipment, construction materials and labour. An excavator on tracks is the best choice for excavating; it has a long reach, enabling it to operate from the side. It is also efficient at moving large quantities of overburden quickly. Bulldozers can do a good job, so long as the subsoil is dry. In moist ground the vibrations from the machine can turn the hardpan to jelly and it is disconcerting to have a bulldozer on quivering ground. JCBs (or backhoes as they are called in North America) are limited by their reach, the size of their bucket and are hard to manoeuvre in soft ground. The excavation and the spreading of the footing will take a day. Allow another day for moving fill, cleaning the site and possibly digging a drainage ditch. To calculate the amount of gravel, multiply the surface area of the water jump by 6in (15cm). A 12ft (3.6m) wide swathe of gravel is necessary around any part of the perimeter that may be ridden on. The amount of geotextile membrane required will also have to be calculated.

Geotextile membrane is expensive. There are situations when it is not required and 6in (15cm) of gravel will, over time, pack to become a firm barrier. However, this synthetic fabric guarantees immediate and long-term good footing. The retaining wall, or revetting as it is called, must be done correctly. If not, the results are like do-it-yourself dentistry – short-term and regretted. Railway sleepers or pressure-treated timber are the most convenient materials to use. Toxic leaching is a concern with pressure-treated timber. Whatever materials are used, they must be resistant to long-term contact with water. There are no short-cuts with revetting and it will take a minimum of three days' labour for the course builder to supervise the excavation and do the revetting. The silver lining in the construction costs is that the mountain of fill excavated can become a bank complex. This gives the organiser two feature fences for the price of one (well, almost).

The construction process is relatively straightforward and, with the exception of the revetting, can be done in a day. This is important because a delay in laying the membrane and spreading the gravel increases the chance of water seeping in and turning the clay into a quagmire. The equipment operator will need the site clearly defined, a plan showing the profile and the course builder on site to assist with shooting sights and supervising. All the materials, including the gravel, must be on site so that there is no idling of expensive excavators. The decision of where to put the fill is governed by practicality and cost. It is best to leave it to dry out for several months before moving it or shaping it into a bank. The mounds of fill should be off to the side of any potential routes to and from the water. It is critical that the base is within one inch of being level; if not it will be difficult to have a consistent shallow depth of water throughout the jump. The excavation should be done by midday; during the lunch break the membrane can be laid out over the base and then the gravel spread in the afternoon.

The depth of gravel is 6in (15cm); this will pack to 4in (10cm). The excavator dumps small piles of gravel, which are then spread with a small tractor and back-blade. The gravel must be packed before the water starts to seep in. A vibrator roller is recommended, but driving backwards and forwards with a tractor is effective in compressing the gravel.

The ramps into the water are done first, and they will require the membrane to prevent the subsoil and gravel becoming mixed. This sloping area between the firm base and the dry land is the most challenging to ensure firm footing. It

DESIGN AND BUILD A **CROSS-COUNTRY COURSE**

Water jump.

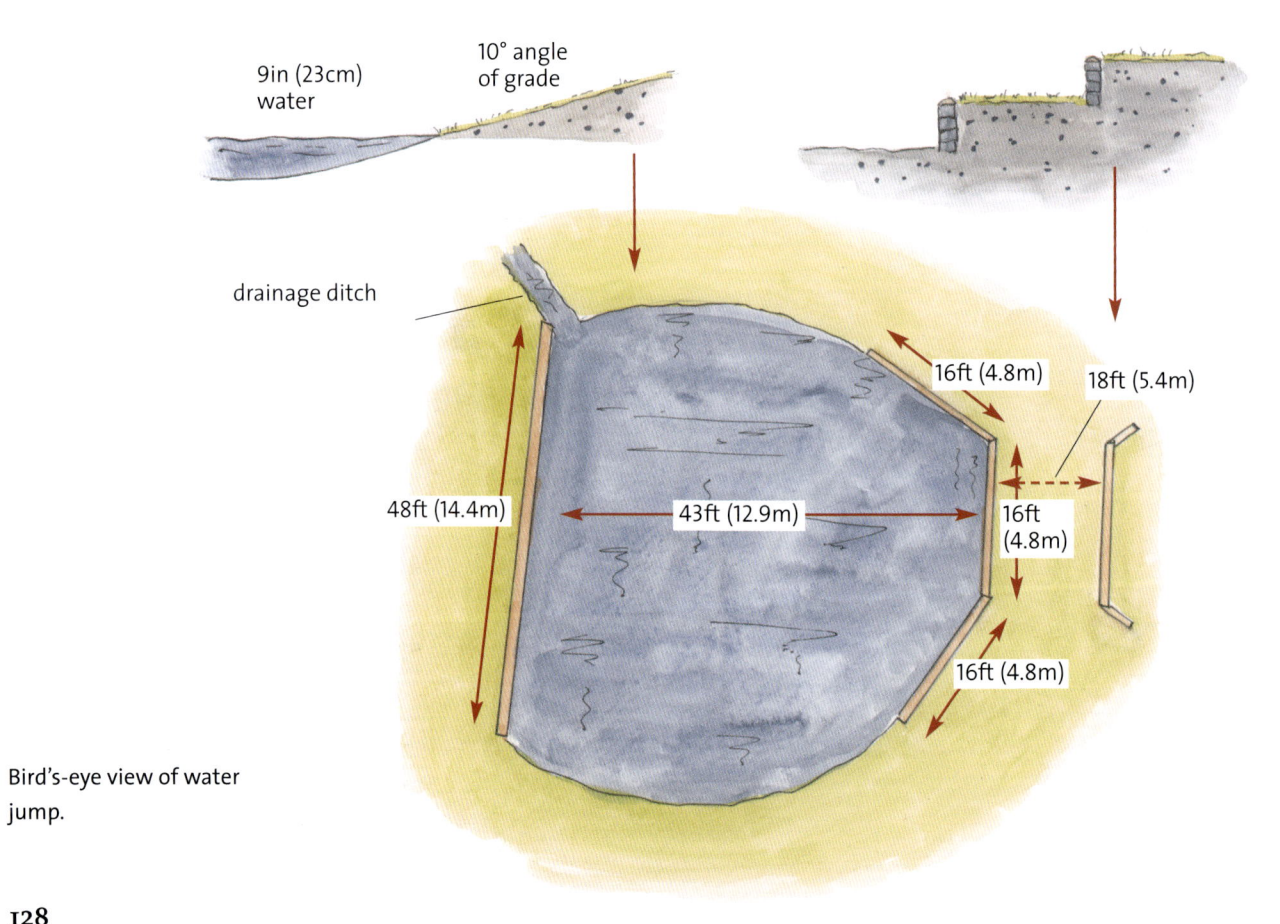

9in (23cm) water

10° angle of grade

drainage ditch

48ft (14.4m)

43ft (12.9m)

16ft (4.8m)

18ft (5.4m)

16ft (4.8m)

16ft (4.8m)

Bird's-eye view of water jump.

128

CHAPTER 11 | WATER JUMPS

may be necessary to build a hardcore base of rock on the exit ramps; these can be finished with a top dressing of screenings. At least the first layer of the revetting should be set in position during the day of excavation. This takes time, as it must be bubble level and built on a firm foundation, such as gravel, rather than oozing mud.

There are three choices of material to use for the footing: pit-run, crusher-run and screenings. I find that 0– ¾ in (0–20mm) pit-run works well. This rounded gravel packs well over time, although it does need occasional raking. If the pit-run gravel has too high a silt content, it will be difficult to pack without a heavy roller. Crusher-run packs the best, but the sharp edges can cut horses' knees if they fall in the water. If it is used, a top dressing of screenings is necessary. Screenings or stone dust is the best choice when money is not a consideration. The drawback is that it has to be packed by a vibrator roller. A cheaper alternative is to do the bulk of the footing with the cheaper pit-run gravel and top it with a dressing of screenings. The revetting must be backfilled with rocks and gravel with a 6in (15cm) top dressing of gravel. This will settle over time and does require periodic maintenance.

Potential problems include depressions forming where horses land and take off, both on land and in the water. Every inch of the base needs to be checked. Generally all that is needed is a little gravel and raking. Holes deeper than a few inches must be filled with rocks and then gravel, and well packed. The edges of the revetting must to be tamped with a digging bar in case there are subsidence

Photo of water jump in previous sketch. *(Photo: Charlotte Harper)*

# DESIGN AND BUILD A CROSS-COUNTRY COURSE

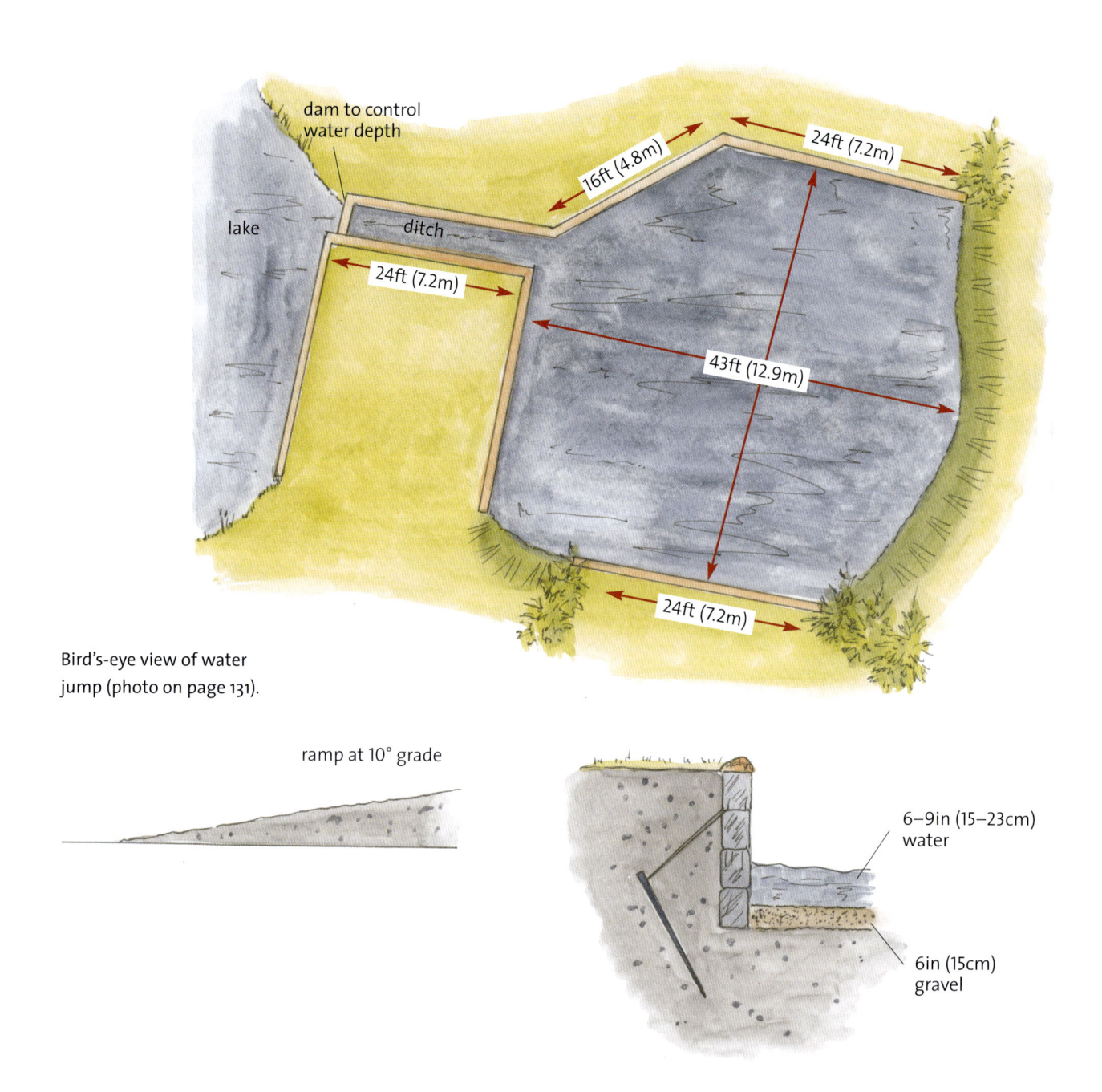

Bird's-eye view of water jump (photo on page 131).

holes; these are then filled.

A drainage ditch or a petrol (gasoline) powered pump will keep the water level to the prescribed 6in–9in (15cm–23cm) depth. A dry water jump is a disappointment, and pointing out that you don't actually have your hands on the

*Water jump used by several levels of competition. (Photo: Charlotte Harper)*

controls of nature doesn't always cut it. There are two options: grab a coat hanger, bend it into a pair of dowsing rods and locate the nearest underground water. Dowsing works so long as you don't think about it. A JCB can dig a 9ft (2.7m) deep sump hole. Lower 3ft (90cm) diameter well tiles into the hole and pack rock around the tiles. Place a concrete cover over the opening. The water that collects can then be pumped into the water jump. The other option is to bring in a water tanker. A note of caution – make sure that you are there when the water is trucked in. If the water is delivered in the pre-dawn darkness on the morning of the competition, it is easy to greet the technical delegate with a reassuring smile, confirming that the water jump does indeed have water. But as the sun rises and the first competitor strides boldly across the water jump, you will not want to witness her collapsing into the chasm cut by the water discharged from the high-pressure hose! Not a satisfactory start to the day. There is a way to take the adventure out of building water jumps and that is by using a liner.

## Building with waterproof liners

Using an impermeable membrane to hold the water is a perfectly feasible option. Environmental agencies use this technology to retain the run-off from mine tailings. The cost is approximately three times that of a water jump with a natural base, and there are no short cuts in the construction process. The

# DESIGN AND BUILD A **CROSS-COUNTRY COURSE**

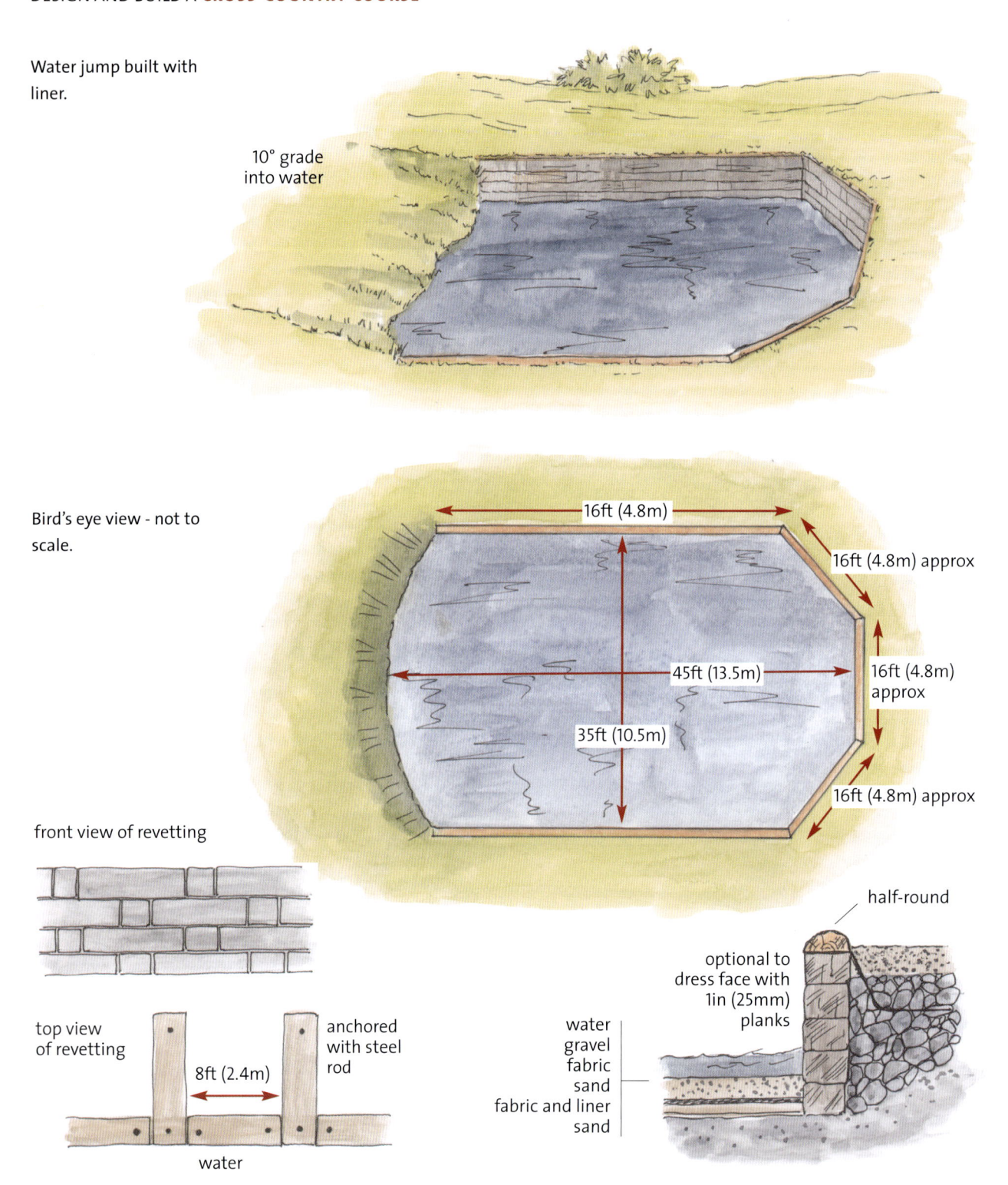

Water jump built with liner.

10° grade into water

Bird's eye view - not to scale.

16ft (4.8m)
16ft (4.8m) approx
45ft (13.5m)
16ft (4.8m) approx
35ft (10.5m)
16ft (4.8m) approx

front view of revetting

top view of revetting

8ft (2.4m)

anchored with steel rod

water

half-round

optional to dress face with 1in (25mm) planks

water
gravel
fabric
sand
fabric and liner
sand

132

CHAPTER 11 | **WATER JUMPS**

advantage is that it can be built anywhere and the level of water is controlled.

- Excavate the site. Check that the base is within an inch of being uniformly level. All stones and irregularities must be removed.

- Revett the sides with pressure-treated 6in x 6in (15cm x 15cm) timber. (Railway sleepers or ties are not recommended for water jumps because of the risk of toxic leaching.) These are pinned together with steel rods every 4ft (1.2m) and tied back every 4ft (1.2m).

- Cover the base with 2in (5cm) of clean sand.

- Cover the sand with a heavy grade geotextile membrane.

- The 0.30mm gauge impermeable plastic material is next. It is best to have it custom made so that it is an exact fit. The alternative is to purchase 12ft (3.6m) wide rolls and then glue the strips together.

Water jump built with waterproof liner. *(Photo: Claus Zander)*

133

- Another layer of geotextile membrane is next. Both the plastic and this layer of fabric come over the top of the revetting and are buried under 12in (30cm) of gravel.

- Two inches (5cm) of sand cover the second layer of fabric. A third layer of fabric is next.

- The final layer is 6in (15cm) of 0–¾in (0–20mm) pit-run gravel or crusher dust. This must be well packed.

- Fit an overflow pipe to control the depth of water.

Every water complex is unique and the jumps around and in the water will depend upon many variables. At the upper levels of competition providing slower alternative routes can cater for the range of abilities. Problems can be expected at the lower levels and it is sad to see the inexperienced eliminated at the water. This can be avoided by having a straightforward jump several strides before the water. A green horse might have one stop, but should jump it on the second attempt. The fence after the water should be more technical and reward those riders who don't abandon the controls with the first splash. Portable jumps give you the flexibility to make changes and adapt the difficulty to fit the day. New water jumps can give everyone, including the builder, the collywobbles prior to the competition. If this is the case then take the reassuring advice of onlookers in the Irish hunt field – 'The devil will leave it, once it's jumped' and get on a horse and take the devil out of it.

## TIPS

- Avoid building a water jump in a stream. Flash floods can tear out revetting, wash the footing downstream and environment agencies can slap you with substantial fines for altering an existing watercourse. However, there may be a clause in local bylaws allowing for a livestock crossing and this might permit a simpler water crossing.

- Avoid the temptation to use one end of a pond or lake. The truckloads of fill required to ensure the shallow water depth of a water jump make this option prohibitively expensive.

- It does make sense to excavate reasonably close to an existing body of water, particularly if it is on slightly higher ground, so that the water level can be controlled by gravity and filled with a pump.

- Revetting is the best way to ensure good footing, but it can be overdone. A rectangular-shaped water jump has few options for future design changes. Two sections of revetting should not join at right angles as this results in an unjumpable section. Instead cut the corner with a third section.

- Geotextile membrane is expensive. I regard it as an insurance policy; it guarantees good footing. It may not be necessary on the base, but it is generally required on the slope into the water, which cuts through the more porous subsoil.

- Used, white styrofoam coffee cups are indispensable in ensuring that the base is within an inch of being level. The excavator operator sits 10ft (3m) off the ground, and asking him to be within an inch (25mm) of level over 100ft (30m) is optimistic. Instead, use the transit to shoot sights and use weighted coffee cups to define areas that are dug to the right depth.

- Laser transits are easy to use and very accurate. They are also very expensive. Excavating contractors generally own high-quality transits, and it is worth asking them to bring one.

- Over time, a layer of ooze and competitor jetsam builds up on the bottom of the water jump. Pump or drain the water out and scrape it clean with the back-blade attached to a tractor. The footing can then be thoroughly inspected and irregularities repaired.

# 12.

# Construction Techniques and Tricks of the Trade

'WHILE THERE'S BREATH, THERE'S HOPE.' That was Sir Ernest Shackleton's response to being stuck on an ice-floe. Now, if you find yourself surrounded by ice ridges and crevasses you probably should have asked for directions a little while back. Nevertheless, there is a frontier ambience to course building and you can find yourself in unsatisfactory

Five indispensable tools (from left to right): digging bar, sledgehammer, peavey, digging clams, and chainsaw. *(Photo: Claus Zander)*

situations. Having a can-do attitude and being a skilled improviser helps to get the job done. This chapter is as much about the everyday tricks and tactics that expand a builder's capabilities as it is about solving problems.

A comprehensive understanding of all the different aspects of design and construction comes from putting your boots on and helping to build courses. Course building is all about digging post holes, working with wood, water and rock, and basic landscaping. Weekend seminars are very useful, but the only way really to learn the business is through an informal apprenticeship with designers and builders.

## Equipment

The list of tools used every day is surprisingly modest, and it is often cheaper to rent the more expensive pieces of equipment that are only used occasionally.

### EQUIPMENT LIST

- Chainsaw (professional size, at least 65 cc with a 20in/50cm bar) (*see safety notes overleaf*)
- Spade, rake, digging bar and digging clams (for removing dirt from postholes)
- 4ft (1.2m) level, 100ft (30m) of nylon line and a line level
- 24ft (7.2m) and 100ft (30m) tape measure
- Axe, sledgehammer and a peavey (for handling logs)
- Power weed trimmer and/or machete
- Cordless drill
- Hammer and assorted hand tools
- Fencing pliers, hacksaw and knife
- Braided nylon rope (3/8 in/10mm diameter), 9 or 10 gauge mild steel galvanised wire, and 1½ in (35mm) staples
- 20ft (6m) logging chain

DESIGN AND BUILD A **CROSS-COUNTRY COURSE**

> ## CHAINSAW SAFETY
>
> The chainsaw has been called the most dangerous tool used by non-professionals. It is the primary tool of the course builder and not only does the everyday work demand great skill, but also work situations can test one's judgement. There are many course-building situations when it is prudent to stop and ask yourself – 'Is this a wise thing to do?' It is essential to take a chainsaw safety course and study the chainsaw owner's manual. Generally these courses take a full two days, and it would be deluding to try to condense the material into a few paragraphs. However, the basic points are:
>
> - Wear the safety gear (steel-toed boots, protective chaps, helmet and gloves).
>
> - Keep the chain sharp and at the correct tension (the bigger the wood chips the sharper the chain).
>
> - Follow the manufacturer's instructions for maintaining and operating the chainsaw.
>
> - Keep bystanders at least 10ft (3m) away from the operator. When logging, the nearest person should be no closer than 2.5 times the height of the tree. It is not recommended that you work alone.
>
> - Kickback, pushback and pull-in are reactive forces that reverse the power of the saw against the operator, i.e. when the upper top tip of the bar touches a log or is pinched, instead of the chain biting into timber, the saw is suddenly flung back towards the user.

In addition, there is a supplementary list of equipment that is used occasionally, such as: generator, logging tongs, block and tackle, and drill attachment for chainsaw.

A tractor with a front-end loader and post-hole auger or post-pounder is considered essential equipment for course building. There are many times when machinery is just not available and you do need to find alternative ways of doing things. Many of these tricks are discussed later in this chapter.

Digging post holes and setting posts in every type of terrain is one of a course builder's most important skills. Post-hole augers and post-pounders represent a huge saving in time and energy, particularly when there are many holes to be dug. However, when there are rocks and other obstructions, it is often quicker to dig by hand. A heavy digging bar will cut through roots and either smash or pry out rocks. Posts must remain firm and true for the life of the jump; if they become loose the jump dimensions can change and the repairs are costly. Post-holes should be 3ft (90cm) deep and the post packed with gravel. (This reduces the risk of frost-heave.) The gravel must be aggressively tamped with a digging bar. The cognoscenti argue about the best tools and materials for tamping posts; essentially it comes down to the effort one puts into it.

> ### PROFESSIONAL'S TIP
>
> It saves considerable time if the fence height can be decided before construction, so that timber has to be cut only once. A mason's line can be used to represent the top rail and give a visual reference. A taut line will also ensure that posts and revetting are straight.

## Ripping logs

Ripping logs into half-rounds is an essential course-building skill, and with a sharp professional-size chainsaw it isn't difficult. Take two blocks of wood and cut a deep 'vee' in both of them. Cradle the log in both 'vees' so that it is stable. Now carefully, and without forcing the chainsaw, let it rip from one end of the log to the other. Stability depends upon the length and weight of the log; hence it is easier to rip a 6ft (1.8m) log, rather than a pair of 3ft (90cm) logs.

## Roping

There are many different styles of course building and a well-thought-out course will recognise the importance of using a variety of building techniques. Safety is the over-riding concern, and any fence that a horse could get caught up in must be built so that it can be quickly dismantled and rebuilt without a change in appearance. Fastening rails to posts with rope is the recommended method. Nylon rope of 5/16in (8mm) or 3/8in (10mm) diameter is best; polyester is the second choice; polypropylene is the cheapest and decays the quickest in sunlight. It is generally best to fasten the ground rail with wire as field mice like chewing on rope. Regardless of the style of roping, the result should be tight, tidy and facilitate the quick dismantling and re-building of the jump.

Here are two methods: the first is quick, simple and cost-effective, while the second is eye-catching and gives an artistic flourish to the finished fence.

- Staple one end of the rope to the post, wrap the rope around the rail (twice is best), draw it tight using the hammer for leverage. Fasten the rope to the post with a pair of 1¾in (45mm) fence staples. Neatly trim off the ends of the rope.

- Stand behind the post with an approximately 12ft (3.6m) length of rope that has a spliced or knotted loop at one end. Pass it behind the post and around the rail on both sides of the post. Pass the end of the rope through the loop, draw it tight and fasten it with a knot. Take the end of the rope and lash together the two strands of rope that are around the post. To create a tight and even lashing, use fencing pliers to grip the rope and snap it into shape with a sharp yank. The added cost of this method, in rope and time, for a complete course is about equivalent to a 12 ton/tonne truckload of gravel.

## Notches

The saddle notch is an easy and simple way to join two logs together or to give a log stability. It is used to build everything from a hog's back to a cabin. Essentially it is little more than a vee cut out of the lower log, which will cradle the upper log. A tight-fitting notch is made by using a pair of dividers or scribes to follow the curve of the upper log and mark this line onto the lower log. The marked area is then cut out by making several close vertical cuts and then chipping these out with an axe. Carefully play the chainsaw over the rough vee-

CHAPTER 12 | **CONSTRUCTION TECHNIQUES**

strain rope with hammer

wrap rope twice around pole

Simple method of roping, using staples.

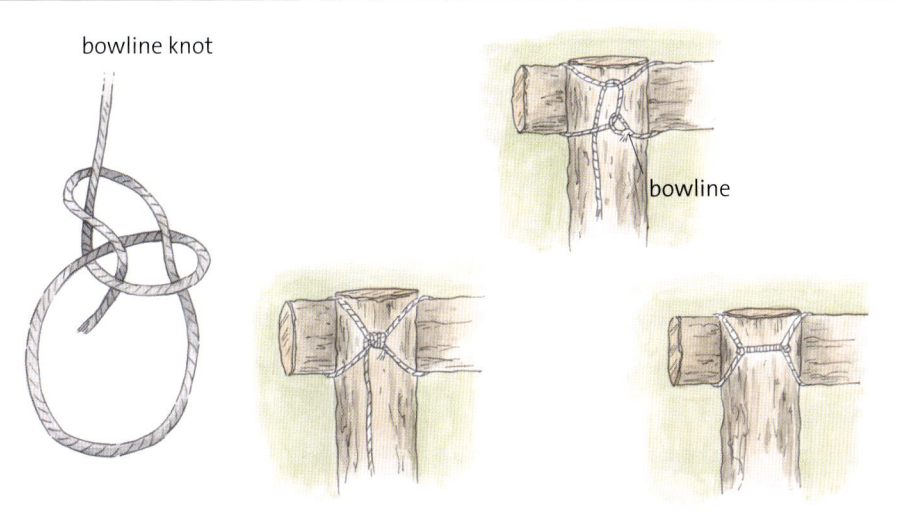

bowline knot

bowline

draw upper and lower loops together to tighten rope

knot and trim end of rope

Alternative method of roping, using lashing.

Saddle notches. Use dividers to scribe a line to match the shape of the top log onto the lower log. *(Photo: Claus Zander)*

shaped notch until it is smooth and round. Place the upper log into the notch, and if the fit is not close enough then remove the top log and trim out a little more until a tight fit is achieved.

Dovetail notches look impressive and are ridiculously easy to do. Their construction technique is described in Chapter 8, under Log Cabins.

## Toe-nailing

Toe-nailing is a simple way of holding two pieces of wood together. Course builders use this method of nailing to hold the railway sleepers together when revetting banks and ditches. Butt the two timbers together and drive a pair of 8in (200mm) nails in diagonally (see illustration page 120). The two timbers are now pinned together. It is easier to do if the nail is held almost vertical until it bites into the wood and then driven in at a 45° angle.

## Revetting

Revetting ditches and water jumps can be a challenge. It may not be practical to dig a post hole for the retaining wall. In this situation use a steel fence post instead of the half-round. A 10lb (5kg) sledgehammer will make short work of minor obstructions. Drive the post in until it is 3in (7.5cm) below the top of the revetting. Take a half-round and cut out a channel in it so that it fits over the steel fence post. Nail the half-round to the revetting.

Occasionally bedrock precludes any kind of post going in the ground. In this case, nail the half-round to the revetting and then double-wire the half-round to the anchor post. One wire passes between the top two layers of revetting and the other passes between the lower two layers of revetting.

If an anchor post is not firm enough there are two options. Either wedge a short length of timber between the anchor post and the revetting or use a 'deadman'. A 'deadman' is a substantial piece of timber buried on the inside of the revetting. It is an effective anchor.

## Moving heavy timber

The next thing to know about is how to handle big timber effortlessly. Telegraph poles are ideal for course building. A tractor with a front-end loader makes it easy to work with them, but it is not essential. In fact, the ability to move and lift

CHAPTER 12 | **CONSTRUCTION TECHNIQUES**

Building portables in winter. *(Photo: Claus Zander)*

logs effortlessly by hand represents a considerable saving in time. A 5ft (1.5m) steel bar, a peavey and the principles of leverage can replace a tractor and assistants. A peavey is a tool used to roll logs. It consists of a loose-fitted hook on the end of a 4ft (1.2m) handle. Here are the simple steps to building a jump using leverage rather than a tractor:

- Using the peavey, roll the 16ft (4.8m) telegraph pole onto a short 6in (15cm) diameter log. When the pole is on one or more short logs, it can then be rolled or swivelled into position. A pair of smooth 4ft (1.2m) small logs are very convenient for rolling logs into position.

Assembling a portable oxer. *(Photo: Claus Zander)*

143

# DESIGN AND BUILD A CROSS-COUNTRY COURSE

- To lift one end of the pole, use the pry bar; or if more leverage is required, place a log under the bar.

- A tree trunk may be simply too big to move, even with leverage. Take a jug of chainsaw bar oil and spread a thin film of oil on the plank or the rail that is under the big log. It will now be easier to slide.

Telegraph poles can be loaded on to a wagon without the use of a tractor. Position the pole so that it is parallel to the wagon and about 6ft (1.8m) from it. Lift the small end onto a log so that it is several inches (cms) off the ground. Bend the knees and lift the small end onto the edge of the wagon. Roll the pole along the edge of the wagon until the point of balance is reached. Prop it up so that it will not roll back and, so long as the point of balance is correct, the heavy end can be flicked up with one hand.

## Felling a tree

Knowing how to fell a tree safely is an essential course-building skill. There are several things to consider before felling a tree, the first being – is there an alternative?

Before cutting down any tree you need to assess: the direction it is leaning, the wind direction, whether dead or broken limbs could fall on the logger, and the likelihood of it getting hung up in other trees.

The procedure is as follows:

- First clear the work area around the tree of brush and other obstructions. Then clear two escape paths. These are opposite to the direction the tree is falling and at about 45°.

- The tree should be cut as close to the ground as possible. Clean dirt off the bark with an axe. If the tree has large buttress roots these have to be cut out.

- A felling notch is cut on the side of the tree that it is intended to fall. This notch is critical and its depth is about a quarter to one third of the diameter of the tree.

- The felling cut is then made on the opposite side and about an inch higher than the felling notch. Never cut through to the notch; instead leave at least an inch (25mm) of hinge.

CHAPTER 12 | **CONSTRUCTION TECHNIQUES**

Felling a tree.

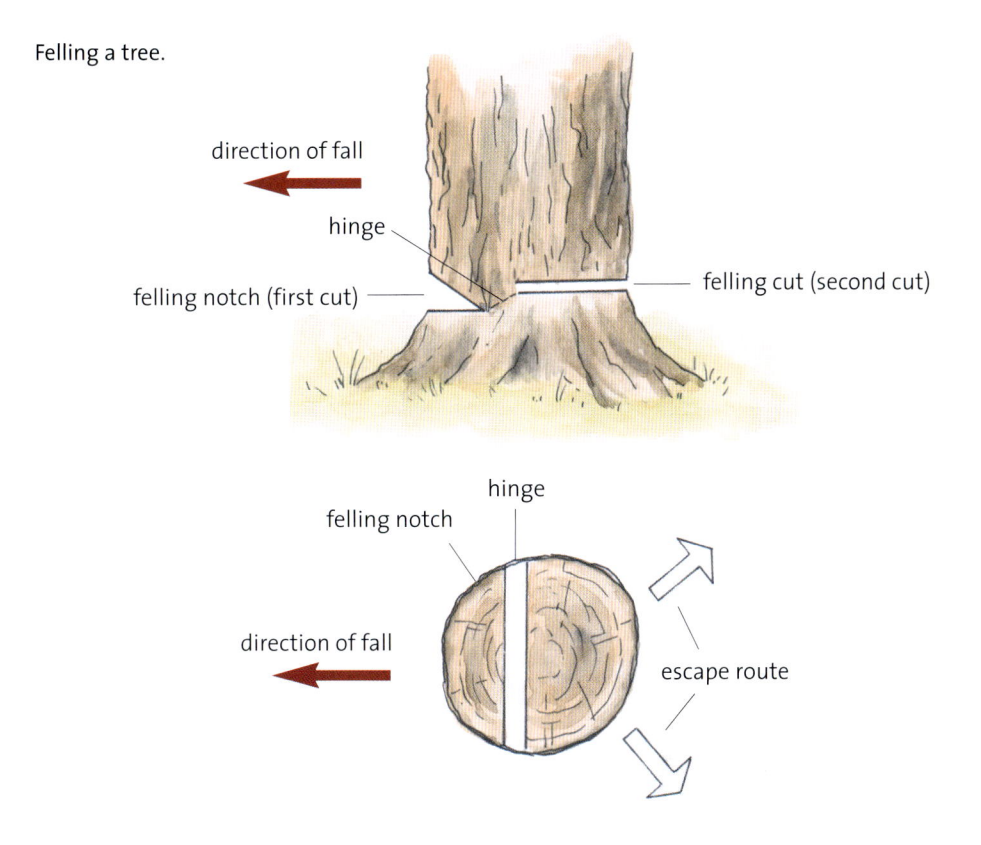

- When the tree begins to fall, get away smartly, with the saw, along the cleared escape route. If it does not fall, then drive a plastic wedge into the cut to control the fall, help tip it over and prevent it falling back in the wrong direction. If the tree does gets hung up, then use a tractor and cable to free it, rather than trying to work under it with the chainsaw. This will help tip it over.
- Limbing off branches can also be hazardous. They can be under tension, and when cut can pinch the saw or spring back at the logger.

## Post holes in awkward places

Digging post holes is done without comment (although you will find a few tips scattered through the book), but you do need to know how to dig post holes in difficult conditions, such as in water, sand, hard clay, bedrock and frozen ground.

If the post hole is for the revetting in a water jump then a steel fence post can substitute for the wooden post and this can be pounded down through the

145

muck and subsoil. A hollowed-out half round can cover the steel post.

Sometimes a post hole can fill with water as soon as it is dug. In this scenario, bail out the water and quickly put the post in the hole, pack a few rocks around the post and empty two bags of dry cement mix into the hole. Tamp it aggressively. The cement mix soaks up the water and the post is firmly set.

A post hole dug in soft sand can look as though it was dug by a dog. Drive a few big nails partially into the end of the post and set the post in concrete mix. Course builders' time is worth more than a bag or two of cement mix.

I learnt how to dig holes in hard ground from an American friend. 'Goddam racq, goddam racq – we do it with water,' he said as the post-hole auger bounced off the rock-hard clay. I assumed the conversation was about the Middle East and wondered aloud what would happen if water bombers were deployed and the enemy had umbrellas. The 'racq' was rock and the water was for the holes. The result was miraculous. If a 6in (15cm) hole is filled with water, even the hardest clay will turn to mud after a few hours. This is then cleaned out and the hole refilled with water. The depth of ground softened is equal to the depth of water.

Digging a hole and hitting bedrock or a boulder just under the surface is no reason to abandon the effort. Widen the hole and securely nail crosspieces onto the end of the post, then set the post in cement.

Digging post holes in frozen ground is a great way of slowing down the neighbours as they drive past. Hot water melts frozen ground as though it were butter.

## Lifting boulders

A big boulder can be lifted out of the ground by using small stones. Dig around and underneath the boulder as much as possible. Lever the boulder so that one or two stones can roll underneath it. Repeat these using progressively bigger stones. The boulder will slowly rise as more stones are levered under it. When it gets to the surface, it can be rolled away.

## Shifting a vehicle that is stuck in mud or sand

Trucks can get stuck in mud or sand. This possibility should not be a deterrent to making full use of a vehicle. It is like having a pencil with an eraser on the end. Mistakes happen, but if the eraser wears out before the pencil then you are probably overdoing it. The main thing is that the delay should be minutes rather than hours. Two essential travelling companions are: a high-lift jack and a pair of 4 ft (1.2m) long, rigid steel mesh racks that can be slid under the wheels for traction. If the tyres are just slipping then these alone are all you need. But if you are buried up to the axle and beyond, then the vehicle will have to be jacked up and a roadway built under it with whatever materials are at hand. Flat rocks and saplings work for light trucks. However, a bulldozer will need railway sleepers and small tree trunks. Dig the muck out and then pack in the timber.

## Using logging chains

Logging chains are useful for more than pulling logs and trucks. For example, when skidding a huge log through dense timber it can get jammed up against the base of a tree. To free it, reposition the hook so that it is half a turn around the log; when the chain is pulled tight it will spin the log sideways. Similarly, if a log that is part of a jump needs to be rotated so that the bow is down rather than up, position the grab hook at the lower side of the log and lift it slowly so that it rotates half a turn.

## Carving with a chainsaw

Although the ability to carve life-size animals for jumps is not a basic course-building skill, these kinds of jumps are becoming popular. Carving with a chainsaw involves using the tip of the bar, and the risk of the chainsaw kicking back at the carver is real. There are two types of carving: three-dimensional figures and reliefs (the faces of gnomes, etc.). The procedure is to take a well-seasoned block of softwood, such as pine or cedar. Cut out the rough shape and then carefully carve and cut the finer details. A deep cut at the back of the figure will help minimise the risk of the figure developing cracks. Lightly burn the finished carving with a blowtorch, then wire-brush the wood clean and stain with a high quality varnish. For more information on chainsaw carving and equipment, go to: www.baileys-online.com

## The stress factor

I would be remiss if I didn't offer some thoughts on the human dimension of course building. Course building for the well-established and prestigious competitions ticks along at an even pace, thanks to good management and planning. But the journeyman course builder lives in a different world, more like a latter-day high plains drifter. He or she may be at a different event every week or two, jumps have to be built, problems fixed and those who are responsible for running the show can be wandering around with the numb shock of disaster victims. The effect of stress can be insidious and debilitating – essentially it robs you of the ability think peripherally and respond quickly to changing circumstances. When you work at an event you become part of a team: the organiser is the team leader. There is an analogy between putting a show together and a mountaineering climbing team. On a mountain slope the leader may have the team rope up together, rather than belay from a secure anchor, but if the leader should slip and fall instead of the less experienced at the lower end of the rope, the whole team can be carried away by the momentum and weight. Park rangers refer to roping up without an anchor as making a mutual suicide pact. Fortunately the effects of a poorly run event are not likely to be so catastrophic but you do need to be aware that people under stress do not function effectively.

## Machinery maintenance

Next to human failure comes machinery failure. Course builders have to be able to make things run and keep them running.

- If chainsaws or weed-eaters are hard to start, the first step is to check the fuel and then clean the spark-plug, air filter and fuel filter.

- To clear a flooded engine, remove the spark plug and pull the starter cord a dozen times. Then warm the spark plug electrodes (the end that goes in the engine) with a cigarette lighter before refitting it. The fuel should be high octane, ethanol-free and have the correct fuel/oil mix.

- Extreme damp or cold weather can prevent a vehicle from starting. If professional help is not available, there are two options. A quick spray of WD40 or hair spray on the spark plugs and wires can overcome damp conditions. However, this does have a fire risk. A battery's cranking power drops with the temperature; the easiest way to warm up the battery is with a hair dryer – but again, this should be done with prudence.

- As well as being able to respond to mechanical hiccups, course builders should also be able to take natural hazards in their stride. This comes down to having an awareness and appreciation of how nature goes about its business and taking the necessary steps so as to avoid becoming part of the food chain.

- Having the ability to improvise is key and I always travel with adhesive tape, a selection of different grades of wire and a packet of whole oats. Oats can plug a leaking radiator as effectively as they do the pangs of hunger.

## Cost-effective ideas

There is a parallel universe out there. For everything that is expensive, new and shiny there is an alternative that is post consumer, cheap or free and readily available. Being cost-effective makes good business sense. Here are some ideas to save money.

- Old tarpaulins or other synthetic fabrics can substitute for geotextile membrane. For an instant repair job of soft boggy footing, lay down the fabric and cover it with 6in (15cm) of gravel. Drive on the gravel to pack it. This surface can be ridden on right away. However, after a few months it can be too firm; in this scenario a sprinkling of peat moss, topsoil or manure shavings will provide a cushion and allow grass to become established.

- Steel culverts and other drainage pipes are expensive. You can make your own culverts by taking a sheet of roofing steel. Roll it into a cylinder and bind it with wire. These 'pipes' are quick and convenient for simple drainage jobs. Stonework hides and covers the sharp ends.

- Losing the topsoil is, to paraphrase Oscar Wilde, not just unfortunate, it's carelessness. Every possible measure needs to be taken to prevent soil erosion. Nevertheless, if the topsoil is gone or if the land is so barren and windswept that it barely exists, you can make topsoil. Spread manure several inches (cms) thick and time and nature will do the rest. Manure that is based on wood shavings or peat moss can be used straight away as a riding surface, although caution is needed in wet weather, as it can cause slippery footing, particularly if it is spread on grass.

- Course building is much easier when you have the right equipment, and that includes a selection of 8in–12in (200mm–300mm) nails. Finding them can be a problem, though. An incredulous shop assistant will invariably question you: 'You want what? What do you want 12-inch nails for?' Explaining what you do only usually opens the door to a 'Pythonesque' exchange. If big nails are not available then go to a welding supplier and order ¼in (6.5mm) mild steel rod and have it cut to the appropriate lengths. If one end is cut at an angle then these make serviceable nails. An alternative is to use ⅜in (10mm) threaded rod, cut it to length with a hacksaw and bolt the timber together. There are drill attachments for chainsaws and these are very convenient and effective.

The tricks of the trade may make the job easier and perhaps help in a difficult situation. But the mark of a professional is defined by two overarching qualities and these are timeless and apply to all construction. Firstly, the builder must have an eye for balance and proportion; and secondly, it is the vigorous application of level, line and measure that ensures that the construction is straight and true.

# 13.

# Pony Club Course Building

THIS CHAPTER AIMS to provide a compact friendly guide for building D and C level courses. The design and construction of these lower level courses is straightforward and uncomplicated. It is better to take advantage of a pony club's inherent reservoir of knowledge and skilled volunteers, rather than spend limited resources on expensive course builders. To get the job done properly, enthusiasm must be ballasted by knowledge. This is not usually a problem, as the gin and jodhpur brigade is never short of sergeant-majors. The first step is to appoint a 'solutions person' who will harness that enthusiasm, and, with a deft touch, direct it with the bridle or the spur as required. Next on the agenda is money and construction materials. Here are some pointers to open the purse strings and load the wagons.

- Potential sponsors respond more positively to requests for product or services rather than cash.

- Explain to prospective donors that this is a one-time request for a new cross-country course. Ask for a relatively small sum, to cover the cost of materials for one specific fence. The sponsor's name will remain on that fence for perpetuity. It will also be included in promotional material. Twenty modest donations are more realistic rather than one major sponsor.

- Capitalise on the goodwill associated with pony clubs and the need of local newspapers for topical local-interest stories. Sponsors appreciate good publicity.

- Angel financing. There are many wealthy people out there who recognise that young people who ride horses are psychologically advantaged over those who do not, and that is good for society as a whole. If you are unsure about how much you dare ask for, try the blink method. Ask for an outrageous sum: if they don't blink, then quickly add that there is also the cost of materials, earthmoving, etc. until you see that you have hit the wall. Every request should be backed with a carefully crafted written proposal.

- Every lumberyard has timber that has been rejected by builders. Design the jumps so that they are built with short lengths of timber.

- Power companies usually say no to requests for used or broken poles. However, the smaller businesses that erect power lines will often stockpile damaged and obsolete poles for a cash sale. Sawmills, demolition yards and arborists are also potential sources of cheap lumber.

- Planning and leadership are essential to avoid the work party unravelling in acrimony and machinery misfortunes. If work, rather than entertainment, is the priority, then it is worth confirming who is coming, what their skills are and then tell them in advance what they will be doing and what tools they should bring. Otherwise you can lose half your workforce for the first hour or two in a caffeine- and testosterone-induced haze of roaring chainsaws and revving trucks as the men compare equipment. The women, meanwhile, will quietly pick up the shovels, rakes and weed-eaters and get on with the job. The key points for supervising work parties are:

    - Only ask people to do what they know how to do.

Surprisingly serviceable jumps can be made from discarded timber. Watch that there are no dangerous gaps between the logs that could trap a foot.

CHAPTER 13 | **PONY CLUB COURSE BUILDING**

Hog's back.

- Be generous with refreshments, but no alcohol on the job.

- Be aware of and follow safety and environmental standards and concerns.

- Recognise and appreciate everyone's effort.

## Building the fences

- Log jumps are the easiest to build and the place to start. Take a log that is not less than 12in (30cm) in diameter and place it on a pair of 3ft (90cm) logs. It is held in place by cutting a round notch in the end logs and then fastened with rope.

- A hog's back is another simple fence to build. It consists of a pyramid of three 8in (20cm) diameter rails that are supported and separated by short logs at either end.

- A similar progression of difficulty can be used when building ditches. The easiest is a shallow rounded ditch (approx. 1ft 6in/45cm) deep and 2ft/60cm) wide) which is defined by revetting on the take-off side. The next

Two examples of easy ditches.

step is a slightly bigger ditch, approximately 2ft 6in (75cm) wide and 2ft (60cm) deep. A cross-pole frame at either end supports a log suspended over the ditch. A ground rail defines the front of the ditch. These examples are fine for small ponies and for getting young horses started, but for a competition a ditch should be revetted on both sides so that long-term good footing is assured.

- Brush jumps are easy and inviting to ride and a safe introduction to bigger fences. The frames are simple to build and consist of a pair of posts set at a slight angle, onto which are nailed two pairs of planks or half-rounds. It is critical that the brush is tightly packed into this frame so that there is no chance of a horse's leg getting caught in the frame. To enhance the ascending profile of the jump pack a roll of brush in front of the frame. A ground rail helps hold the brush in place and defines the front of the jump.

- Stone walls add variety and at these levels of competition the masonry skills are undemanding. To protect horses' legs the top of the wall should be wood not stone. The easiest way to do this is to set a pair of posts for either end of the wall and wire a short support post to the front side of the post. Place a rail on the supports and rope it to the posts, then build the wall under this rail. The joins between the stones should all be crossed and the rocks fitted so that they all lean in toward the centre of the wall. It is usually necessary to anchor a ground rail on the take-off side so the fence has an ascending profile.

- Tyre jumps tend to be associated with run-down backyard paddocks and consequently some people look askance at them. This is unfortunate because tyres are free and they make excellent jumps – so long as they are well built. The construction is straightforward. Set a pair of posts in the ground

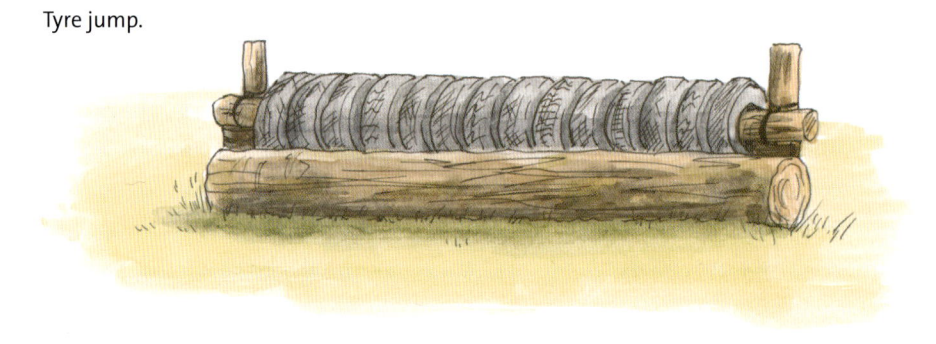

Tyre jump.

CHAPTER 13 | **PONY CLUB COURSE BUILDING**

Hanging log. *(Photos: Claus Zander)*

Park bench.

Ascending rails.

155

DESIGN AND BUILD A **CROSS-COUNTRY COURSE**

Simple bank.

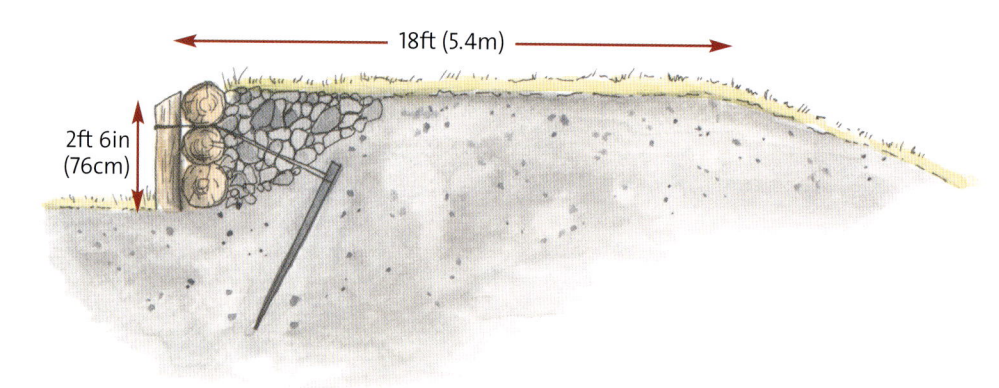

2ft 6in (76cm)

18ft (5.4m)

14ft–16ft (4.2m–4.8m) apart. Wire support posts to the posts in the ground and place a 7in (17.5cm) diameter rail on these support posts. Rope one end of the rail to the post and then string the tyres on the rail. It is critical that the tyres are immovable and present a solid and gap-free face. This is done by suspending the tyres just off the ground. Packing the last few tyres on the rail can be a challenge as you have to hold up the tyre-laden rail as you thread on the tyres. A hi-lift jack or a front-end loader tractor may be necessary. Having the tyres tightly packed and suspended just off the ground combines to create a solid, immovable fence. A log on either side further ensures that they cannot move and also gives the fence an ascending profile.

- Banks are an essential component of every course and, like ditches, are the nucleus of combinations and schooling fences. The simplest bank is little more than a 2ft 6in (75cm) step onto an earth bank or berm. Cut one side of

Ramp.

CHAPTER 13 | **PONY CLUB COURSE BUILDING**

Flowers add a flourish. Left, a flower box with trellis roof; and above, a palisade with flowers. *(Photos: Charlotte Harper)*

the bank so that it has a straight edge. Stack three 10in (25cm) diameter logs against this edge. These logs are held in place by a pair of posts that are wired back to an anchor post on the inside of the bank. The logs should lean in slightly toward the bank and must be backfilled with rocks and gravel.

- It is important that these lower-level courses have variety and do not appear to be just a collection of log and rails. Flower-box jumps are simple to build and add colour. There are several different construction methods. The simplest is to build a rectangular box that is approximately 14ft (4.2m) long

Flower box – alternative design. *(Photo: Charlotte Harper)*

157

Log and rocks.

and 2ft (60cm) high. These jumps are an opportunity to reflect the heritage of the region. For example, a saddle notch for logs, and lap or dovetail join for squared beams. A rectangular frame that is approximately 3ft (90cm) wide and 2ft (60cm) high is first built. This is then filled with topsoil and a log is positioned across the top of the box. The top log makes the fence ascending from both directions, and if the fence is positioned on a slope it can be used by two levels of competition. Real flowers are wonderful if they are donated, but good-quality synthetic varieties have many advantages.

- A common design technique is to build straightforward jumps – such as a cordwood or stone wall – in the fence lines and then add ascending rails on a bending line several strides away. The lower level can jump just the cordwood in the fence line, while the higher level jump both fences. The feature fences, such as pens and banks, should be out in the open so that they can be ridden from four directions. The goal is to have as many fences as possible not only ridable from both directions, but also by different levels of competition. This can be done by building jumps with an adjustable top rail and siting jumps on a slight rise so that they are higher on one side than the other. The more fences are jumped, the better and more resilient the footing will become, so long as it is strengthened with gravel and regularly maintained.

## Walking a course

Pony Club courses are all about learning and having fun or, as William Butler Yeats so nicely said – 'education is not filling a bucket, but lighting a fire'. But that fire can splutter if one essential skill is not learned, namely: how to walk a course.

The way **not** to walk a course is to start at the beginning and go from fence to fence, stopping at each one and analysing its qualities, like a tourist at an art gallery. No, the way to walk a course is to stop fifty feet (15m) before the jump and think about what your first impression is. By visualising what the horse sees, rather than what the spectator sees, you have a better chance of sending enthusiasm rather than anxiety down the reins. This does not mean that you don't need to thoroughly evaluate every aspect of the jump and its surroundings. You do. But it is how you present your horse to the fence that really matters, and that will be influenced by what the horse sees three or four strides out. When you walk a course you are also buying a product. If you do have concerns, now is the time to address them to your coach, the riders' representative or the technical delegate. Bear in mind that just as you must visualise the jumps from a horse's perspective, you also need to appreciate that the sport is fuelled by altruism and may have a newly minted technical delegate gripping the controls.

## Jump judges

There is also a wild card, and it comes with a lawn chair. Jump judges at established events are paragons of fortitude and wisdom. But as you travel to the margins, the influence of the horse trials haji diminishes and you can find that the sport is provided by a character like Owen Monet. He recently switched from tillage to building cross-country courses, driven by a zeal that he will be soon be baling the dough. His neighbours have also abandoned the furrow for the video store and assume that a horse trial is the mafia's answer to a bad day at the races. They gladly fill the ranks of the volunteers in anticipation of a day's jovial camaraderie. So if your clear round looks like a bingo score, take consolation in that a good story endures while ribbons and rosettes fade.

# 14.

# Short Course Eventing, Hunter Trials & Team Chasing

Changes in society are being mirrored by the changes in equestrian sport. There is a levelling of hierarchies and an independent spirit that has an eye on the bottom line rather than conforming to old formalities. A generation or two ago, horse shows were run by relics of the squireocracy. Their largesse and inherent knowledge are now largely replaced by equestrian centres that see the business opportunities in people's passion for riding cross-country. As equestrian sport evolves there are two points to bear in mind: diversity gives strength, and one can be short-sighted by tradition. There has always been a myriad of related cross-country sports that have quietly thrived on the margins. Here is a brief outline of three cross-country sports: two of them go back to the mists of time while the other is still in its infancy.

## Short course eventing

Imagine having a horse trials where the entry fee, cross-country construction costs, number of volunteers and the time schedule were more than halved. That describes short course eventing and, like no-frills airlines, it may well soon grow from niche to mainstream. It consists of a dressage test followed by a combined show jumping and cross-country course over a modified course. The jumping course begins and finishes in the show jumping ring, but the middle section consists of a loop of cross-country jumps.

The distance is considerably shorter than a normal cross-country course and it is designed so that, if possible, every fence can be seen by the judge in the show jumping ring. Only one horse is on course at a time and consequently only two judges are required: one for dressage, and the other for jumping. In practice, some of the cross-country fences, such as banks and other combinations, will require jump judges. Competitors are not timed, and a well-thought out jumping course controls the speed. The benefit for riders is that this is a great schooling and tune-up opportunity in a competition format that does not put wear and tear on the pocket book or horses' legs. For organisers, 'eventing unplugged' is simply a less complicated and alternative way to do business and provide sport. Recommended distances and guidelines are outlined in Appendix A.

## Hunter trials

Hunter trials, or cross-country trials as they are also known, are about having a good time, rather than improving oneself and one's horse. Instead of a rigid structure of rules, this sport is guided by the principles of horsemanship and the spirit of a good gallop across a line of country. These courses sometimes may look a little rough around the edges, but when well built they ride like music frozen in time and place. It is up to the riders to decide the melody and rhythm; they can rock and roll for the fastest time and take all the brave routes, or waltz round in the pairs division.

There are usually at least two levels of course, and their standard and appropriateness should be comparable to the levels of horse trials so that riders have a frame of reference. The competition is divided into different divisions, such as: pairs, junior, adult, singles and teams. The pair's division is the first to run and this serves as a warm-up round for the less experienced. A surcharge for late entries encourages riders to make their entries in advance. This assists with the scheduling and planning. The ambience is informal and the starter's assistant plays a key role in hustling competitors from the warm-up ring to the start box.

The course should be inviting, straightforward and challenging enough to tickle riders, but it should not require the technical riding of a typical event course. The course builder needs to keep in mind that poor riding and unfit horses can be expected. The broader the scope of riding abilities, the more carefully thought out the design should be. It should restrain those who like to 'ride 'em on their belly' and look after those who enjoy a loose rein and have a slight inability to worry properly. This is done by carefully siting the fences so that if the horse gets to the fence, it will jump regardless of what the rider is or isn't doing, but if the rider does not ride the course, a few run-outs or circles are probable.

The business of having jump judges fill out result sheets and then have a runner collect them is fraught with risks and belongs to the days of the Boer War. A better way is for jump judges to radio the results in as they happen. If there are two riders on the course at the same time, then two scorers can monitor the radio. To be most effective one person will report on two or three fences. Hard copy results are kept by the jump judges in case of disagreements. Ideally there will be a jump judge at every fence, but in practice one person can often cover several fences. However, it is important that all the fences can be seen by someone with a radio. The fairest way to decide the optimum time is to average all the times and then take the time that is nearest to the average. Time penalties are incurred for riders who are either too fast or too slow. One second equals one penalty point. An interesting twist to the competition is to have bonus points on one of the more challenging fences. For example, by jumping the Corner, a rider gains 25 bonus points, as opposed to the minus 20 points for a refusal. This can give the winning edge to the hardcore and gives the decision making to those in the saddle.

## Team chases

Reins slipping from rain and sweat, the ring of irons clashing, rat-tat-tat of flying hooves clipping the top rail, a fusillade of mud stinging the face and creak of leather straining to counterbalance the nose dive. Team chases fill the gap between hunter trials and point-to-points, and they have a reputation for hard-riding recklessness. This is unfortunate because they are easy to organise, and with option fences and an optimum time division they can be a Sunday afternoon sport for all the family. The course is roughly 2–3 miles (3–5km) long with about twenty fences. It should be over a natural line of country, with the fences looking as though they belong in the landscape. The jumps should be not less than 16ft (4.8m) wide and built to be ridden at speed.

There are two types of team chases: one has sponsorship and attracts competitive teams, while the other has several categories and attracts a wider range of riders. The lower level may be restricted to ponies and young people, and this enables families to enter as a team with the parents jumping the bigger fences and the children popping over the smaller fences alongside, or perhaps vice versa if the parents are the wobblers. Having different categories, such as fastest and optimum time, reduces the risk of riders galloping fast over small fences.

The structure of the sport is straightforward. The rules may vary slightly, but essentially each team has four riders and the time of the first three riders past the post decides the result. The jumps are built in fence lines wherever possible and this facilitates having slower options. These easier jumps are sited so that the added distance will result in time penalties.

The fences should be characteristic of the locality. Regardless of whether brush or timber fences predominate, the basic principles of course design must be followed. All the jumps should have a well-defined ground and top line and have an ascending profile. The footing will probably need to be strengthened on either side of the jumps and potential hazards taken care of. For example: brush jumps must not have a hidden back top rail, and stone walls should be capped with sod or timber and possibly have a roll of brush or a rail in front. Water jumps are great for excitement; however, they should be more of a galloping splash-through than a serious question. Post and rail fences can be built so that the risks of riding them at speed are mitigated. Build the fence with a slight lean. The lower three or four rails are approximately 8in (20cm) in diameter, but the top rail is only 4in (10cm) in diameter and made of a softwood, such as pine or cedar. This enables it to break rather than cause a fall. It must be securely roped, though, so that when it breaks it does not fly in the air and become a hazard. A roll of brush on the take-off side goes a long way towards helping horses stand back and clear the jump.

## Principles not rules

Hunter trials and team chasing come from an earlier sporting tradition that grew from the challenge and excitement of being able to cross a line of country on a good horse. That tradition is rooted in principles of horsemanship and sportsmanship. Consequently, the rules that are written for these sports are more of a pragmatic way to provide structure and allow the organisers to rein in the incorrigible. The operation of these, perhaps unregulated, sports must be at or above industry standards. These standards are available on the internet and can help keep you from getting caught in the cross hairs of the barristocracy. People like certainty, and advance publicity must be informative and accurate.

This includes stating the level of medical and veterinary response available on the site. Every competition will need to write its own rules, but here are six principles worth considering:

- The organisation, operation and the cross-country course are at or above industry standards.

- Competitors are stakeholders in regard to safety and must recognise their limitations.

- The organising committee will decide upon all disputes and decisions.

- Hard hats must meet current industry certification standards and are mandatory, as are riding boots. Body protectors are recommended.

- Abusive riding or behaviour will result in disqualification.

- The committee has complete authority over every aspect of the competition and will make decisions that best reflect the spirit of the sport.

# 15.

# Cross-Country Fences for Training Centres

Planning cross-country jumps for training centres must be as carefully thought out as those for competition courses. The jumps are the same, but instead of being set as a linear course, they are arranged as a series of hubs or groups of half a dozen fences in close proximity. These fences should ride from both directions and be usable in every possible permutation. The focus of each hub is a natural feature, such as a bank or ditch, around which are carefully sited portables and fences with adjustable heights. The objective is for the coach to be in the centre of the action and direct each schooling session as the situation demands. Apart from being practical for coaches and riders, these hubs make the best use of scarce land and cash. Look at the site with an open mind. Moist, wet ground could be scooped out to become a simple water jump, or an outcrop of bedrock framed up to become the base of a bank. The objective is to make use of what was previously unproductive. Training centres are businesses, after all, rather than simply purveyors of sport.

The overall plan should reflect how the fences are going to be used and the goals of the training centre. There is a subtle difference between designing groups of fences for training horses as opposed to having the emphasis on teaching riders. The open area is kept for the teaching riders, so full use can be made of bending lines and learning how to establish a rhythm and jump at a cross-country pace. An open wooded area lends itself to introducing horses to cross-country. The paths between the trees become jumping lanes. The fences are usually straightforward logs and rails that can be ridden at a trot.

Paddock fence lines are potential sites for jumps; a roll top with a slip rail over it works well in this situation.

The principal fences to build first are ditches, banks and steps, followed by an assortment of log and spread fences. Portable jumps, such as a hog's back, flower box, portable oxer and roll top, all work well as the satellite jumps around the feature fence.

# 16.

# Land Management

This is a topic that might seem superfluous in a book on course building. Not so – the perception might be that cross-country courses are a slightly exotic variety of rural artwork found in ancestral parks. The reality is very different. A more common scenario would have the course builder summoned to a recently purchased rural property that its owner proclaims is perfect for a course. It may well be, one day. But first there is the tangled mass of swamp, uprooted trees and rock outcrops to contend with. The first job is to reconcile the site's natural attributes and the requirements of a course. This means building roads, bridges, and improving drainage with a nod to stewardship and preserving habitat. Even if the course builder does not do the work, he or she should understand the principles and be able to give good advice.

## Road building

The two main principles of road building are that the road must have a good foundation and surface water must drain off to the side and not down the length of it. On level ground the roadway is built up higher than the surrounding land and a shallow drainage ditch is dug on either side of it. On a hill, the road should be cut diagonally down the hill and graded so that surface water runs to a ditch dug on the inside between the road and the higher ground. A culvert under the road will drain this water away. Building a road across soft ground can take a prodigious amount of rock to make the foundation. A simpler alternative to rock

# DESIGN AND BUILD A CROSS-COUNTRY COURSE

Side view of road traversing a hillside.

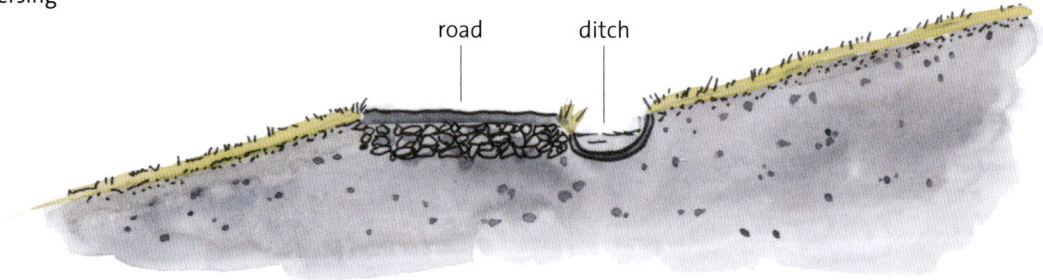

Ditches and culverts prevent roads being washed out.

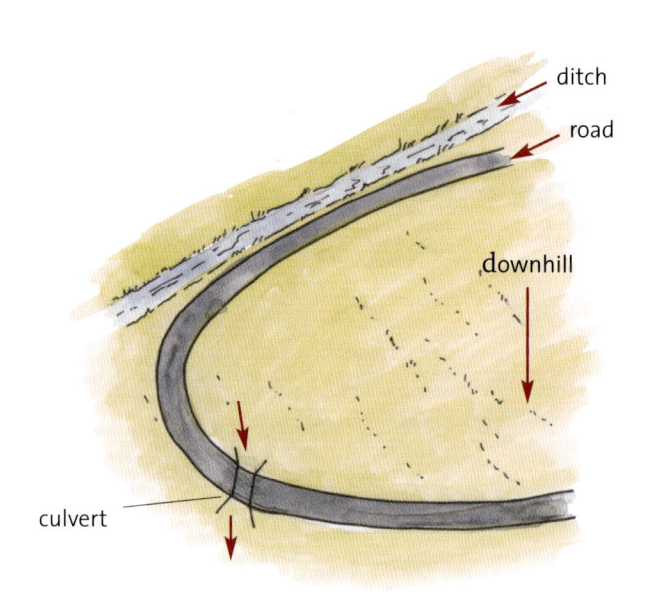

is to build a corduroy road. Lay logs and tree limb across the track, cover it with a geotextile membrane and add 6in (15cm) of gravel. This will set to become a firm road surface. It is easiest to spread the gravel twice as thick as it needs to be and grade it down gradually. This gives you a stable surface to work on.

## Drainage

Drainage should also be considered if the course has to cross wet ground.

The world of ditches is one of contradictions. A dry ditch is a successful ditch – it works because the water has drained out of it; as opposed to a wet ditch, which is water with nowhere to go. To drain a wet hillside the ditch is dug across the upper side of the hill, rather than just across the bottom of the hill. This prevents water from flowing down the hillside. Merely digging a ditch

CHAPTER 16 | **LAND MANAGEMENT**

across the lower part of a wet hillside will only collect water that has soaked the ground: it does not prevent water-logging. To do this a herring-bone pattern of field tile will also likely be necessary, especially if springs across the hillside are the cause of the wet conditions. The drainage tile should be deep enough so that it is below the frost line and have a minimum fall of not less than 1:100. The most critical part of drainage is the outflow end of the drainage tile. There must be sufficient fall in the land for the water to flow freely from the pipe; if not, it will soon become blocked with sediment.

There are only two warm-blooded species on this planet that have the skills to change their environment so that they can live successfully – us, and the beaver. Both implement water-management plans. However, the beaver, unlike some of us, has a better work ethic when it comes to controlling water. The key requirements for site managers are to reduce the velocity of storm water and direct its flow so that water-logging and flood damage are prevented. For example, if the site is in a bowl there are several levels of protection that can be

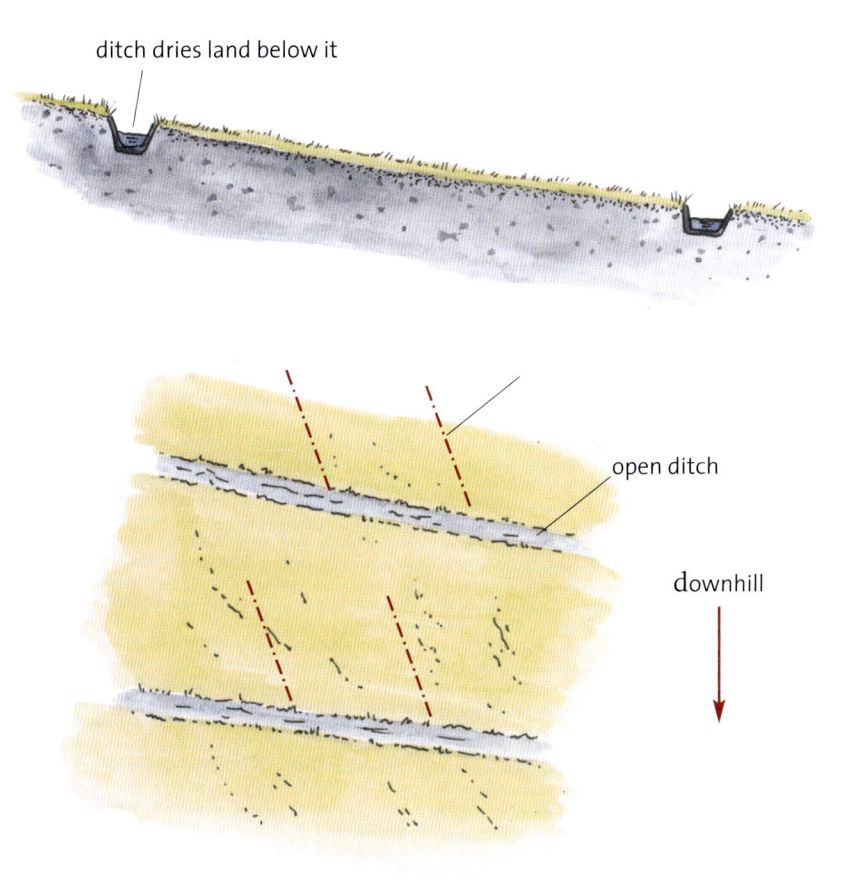

A ditch can drain the land both above and below it.

169

implemented to mitigate the effects of torrential rain. Water can be prevented from flowing down a hillside by building a series of low earth berms. These parallel the contour of the land and direct surface water to a holding pond lower down the hill. In dry weather this pond is empty, but it has the capacity to hold the run-off from several inches (cms) of rain. An open ditch drains the pond and this empties into a storm drain. Boulders can be used around the edge of the storm drain to dissipate the velocity of the water.

## Bridge building

Bridge building is not complicated – it just requires the right material and workmanship so that it lasts for many years. Pressure-treated power poles or 16ft (4.8m) railway sleepers are ideal. Posts are set deep in the ground; a pair of cross members are bolted to the posts. A 3ft (90cm) length of ⅝in (16mm) threaded rod is ideal for bolting the timbers together. The deck can be made of 6in x 6in (15cm x 15cm) pressure-treated beams. A 6in (15cm) dressing of stone dust or gravel will provide a good riding surface. Another option is to use the deck of a flat-bed truck or trailer and cover it with gravel.

If a water jump is made from one end of a lake, or if the course uses a causeway across a pond, then it may be necessary to construct guard rails across a section of open water. Digging post holes and setting posts in open water is challenging but perfectly feasible. Setting the post in a cement-filled container is another option. The trick to avoid the structure looking as though it belongs in a mangrove swamp is to run a wire cable through the posts. Drill a hole through the tops of the posts, thread a steel cable through the holes and fasten it to braced anchor posts on land. A turn-buckle can be used to tension the cable until it is taut and this holds the posts in position. Guard rails are then bolted to the posts and these make the cable less visible.

# 17.

# Risk Assessment and Crisis Management

Since neolithic times, horses and people have had a close relationship that has benefited both. The risks and benefits of this relationship have long been recognised and accepted. Which way the balance tilts depends upon knowledge, skill and chance.

However, in recent years this balance has shifted by the growth of government and its agencies at the expense of individual freedom. This affects all aspects of our lives, including equestrian sport. The concept of 'common good' as decreed by experts is taking precedence over individual decision making. Some risk-takers think that they no longer have to take responsibility for their actions, or worse, they use hindsight as a malevolent gift to seek retribution. Living in the shadow of litigation chill is an unpleasant reality, but there are strong moral, ethical as well as financial reasons to do everything possible to prevent accidents.

There are no guarantees of safety in any human endeavour. Equestrian organisations struggle over what level of risk is acceptable and how it can be reduced. However, psychologists overwhelmingly agree that not only is risk good for you, it is an essential ingredient to keeping us firing on all cylinders.

The alternative to scrapes and bruises is the slow suicide of sedentariness. One of the challenges facing those of us involved in providing horse sport is that the dangers appear to outsiders as quantitative and tangible. The emotional, mental and physical benefits of riding are more intangible and hard to quantify. To further complicate the issue, the sport has to accommodate the wonderful untidiness of humanity. What is the best way of instilling self-monitoring skills in all the stakeholders? The stupid stay stupid because they don't know they are stupid. Regardless of one's viewpoint on how much people should be responsible for their own actions, if you are providing a service or activity involving risk, then society expects you to show due standards of care. To do that, you will need a risk management plan and understand how accidents happen.

In the search for the cause of falls, and what constitutes an unsafe fence, it is easy to get lost in the low cloud of looking at it from the micro level. The picture becomes clearer if a broader view is taken. Both industry and adventure tourism have done surveys, kept statistics and identified the general causes of accidents. These can be applied to equestrian sport. Essentially, accidents are caused by a combination of outside and human factors and as these increase, the risk multiplies. The key points are:

- Accidents are usually caused by an accumulation of little things that create a domino effect.

- Most accidents result from people doing unsafe things.

- On average there are three hundred 'close calls' before that same unsafe act causes a serious injury.

- The seriousness of the accident largely comes down to chance. The occurrence may be preventable.

- The on-site supervisor of the activity is the key person in accident prevention.

The next step is to apply this to horse shows. There are three wild cards that organisers can expect – loose horses, adverse weather and personnel disappointments. Preventing loose horses from running down spectators or getting out on the road is best addressed through site planning. Just as ships have watertight bulkheads to prevent flooding, so gates and other barriers are needed to prevent loose horses running amok. This particularly applies to the cross-country course. One way of doing this is by having gates that can be closed quickly when the PA system or the radio network alerts everyone to the loose horse.

Warm-up rings are frequent sites for accidents. Injuries caused by kicks are all too common when too many horses and people are in the close proximity. An unexpected delay in the schedule can result in a back up in the warm-up ring.

This requires on-the-spot monitoring and supervision.

Weather extremes also need to be factored into the site and show plans. Hot, dry weather can result in slippery footing and the risks of dehydration. Wet weather can prevent vehicular access to all parts of the course. Every fence must be accessible by an ambulance. A protocol should be established to respond to thunderstorms and lightning.

Personnel disappointments can blind-side you. Do not be critically understaffed, recruit the best and never assume anything. Detailed planning and an excellent communication system will go a long way towards preventing accidents.

Having a risk assessment plan helps in identifying potential problems. Every such plan has to be tailored to the individual demands of the competition or business. It should include the following elements.

- Description of the business or activity.
- Risk management objectives.
- Identifying the risk potential to people, the activity and the site.
- Evaluating the risks.
- How to control and manage the risks.
- Insurance coverage.
- Official and volunteer qualifications and training, competitor information, site preparedness and facilities.
- Crisis response strategy.
- Appendix of forms (accident/incident report, incident information log, parent/guardian call form, media release).

Even if you do everything right all the time, the reality is that bad things can happen. The immediate cause of an accident may be outside your control, but with advance planning and preparation you can influence its outcome. Crisis management is about planning for a worst-case scenario.

The first step is to prepare a written crisis response protocol and a master file of all the officials and participants. There is a raft of forms that must be readily available – accident/incident report form, parent/guardian call form, medical form of participants, and media release. The next step is to assign personnel to form a Crisis Response Team and appoint their leader and spokesperson. The team will coordinate information gathering, assess the seriousness of the crisis, its effect on the individual, other participants and the related community. It should also assess the level and type of intervention by organisational support services, such as equestrian associations, lawyers, insurance agents and others. In short, the team takes charge and needs to know what to do. Here is a generic list of those protocols:

- Assess the situation and the seriousness of the injuries.
- Call for emergency medical response and other emergency personnel as required.
- Obtain the names and addresses of any witnesses.
- Document the details of the accident, including location, time, description of activity, injuries, etc. (facts only).
- Draw a picture or take a photograph of the accident location.
- Complete an accident report, make notes of pertinent information and forward it immediately to the next level of authority.
- Contact your insurance broker.

Risk and crisis management are contentious issues that are constantly evolving. But there is one constant: if you are involved in providing an activity that has inherent risk, there are four things expected of you:

**1.** Be able to show due diligence and responsibility for managing risks during the planning and operation of the activity.

**2.** Be responsible for mitigating these risks as much as possible.

**3.** Respond adequately to incidents that occur as a result of the activity.

**4.** Demonstrate due standards of care. This has been defined as having the moral qualities, judgement, knowledge, experience, perception of risks and skill that a person in the capacity of a professional would have.

# 18.

# Falling with Style

Uncertainty is part of the overall order of things, and if you ride horses that uncertainty follows you like your shadow. The problem is that many riders have a fatalistic attitude to falling: if it happens, it happens and they hope for the best. This is a big mistake – just as you control what your shadow does, you can also take control of the uncertainty of falling. That does not mean that you can prevent the fall, but rather how you hit the ground; and it is upon this that the severity of the injury will depend. The people who have turned this into an art form are the members of the stunt industry. One of the types of falls that trainee stunt people are taught is the head-on bike crash into a solid object. The trick to doing this successfully is to have your upper body leaning slightly to the right or left at the moment of impact. The impact then throws you to the side so that the fall is absorbed laterally across the shoulder and back in a neat tuck-and-roll movement, rather than be thrown head first. To stay centred on the bike as it hits the barrier is akin to diving into an empty swimming pool.

I have to admit that I once dabbled in dressage, but I stopped before it became a problem. However, I do recall how much centred riding is regarded as a basic tenet. I have watched many falls over the years and it is noticeable how show jumpers and jockeys who tend not to be centred over the horse's neck often walk away after doing a somersault.

But the high standards of equitation in eventing today have resulted in less 'seat-of-the-pants' riding in favour of a more perfect centred style. Unfortunately riding deep in the saddle and with a long stirrup does not give you the flexibility to respond quickly if the horse hits a fence hard. The tricks that stunt people learn so that they fall effortlessly, are also taught at local gyms; in fact, all the martial arts as well as gymnastics teach the same tuck-and-roll technique until it becomes second nature. By mastering the art of falling with style you can ride off into the sunset with the shadow of uncertainty galloping along upsides.

# Glossary

APRON: A tightly packed roll of brush on the take-off side of a steeplechase fence.

BLACK FLAG: Refers to a recent rule change affecting how option fences are built and flagged on a cross-country course. In the past option and alternative fences were often either attached to or in close proximity to the fast-route fences. It is now recommended that there are at least three strides between these types of fences. This is so that it is more likely that horses will be properly presented to a fence after a run-out. The flags of these jumps have a diagonal black stripe across them.

CAMBER: Positive camber describes a track surface that is lower on the inside of a turn than the outside; negative camber is the opposite.

CRUSHER-RUN GRAVEL: Sharp-edged gravel that is produced by passing rock through a crusher mill. The material is graded into various sizes by being passed through different size screens.

GEOTEXTILE MEMBRANE: The generic name for a woven synthetic fabric. This permeable material is used to keep gravel separate from the underlying subsoil.

PEAVEY: A tool for rolling logs. It works on the principle of leverage: a free-swinging hook grips the log and the 5ft (1.5m) handle provides leverage.

PIT-RUN GRAVEL: Rounded gravel from alluvial deposits.

REVETTING: The retaining wall that supports the sides of ditches, steps and banks.

RIPPING: Technique of cutting a log lengthwise with a chainsaw. The two pieces are called half-rounds.

Rip-rap: 5–6in (12.5–15cm) diameter rock.

Scalpings: The next size up from stone dust or screenings. It essentially has the same properties as stone dust, and all these finer grades are interchangeable.

Screenings: The finest grade of crushed stone, also known as stone dust.

Striding: Refers to the distance between two jumps in terms of a horse's stride, e.g. the striding is too long.

Washed gravel: Gravel that has been separated into different grades by washing it through different size screens. Not recommended for footing applications because it is the mix of different sizes that gives gravel its binding properties.

# Appendix A

## Guidelines for Short Course Eventing

*by kind permission of Sue Collins, Foggy River Farm*

This sport bridges the gap between a combined test (dressage and show jumping) and horse trials, and consists of a dressage test followed by a combined show-jumping and cross-country course. The jumping phase begins and finishes in the show-jumping ring with a middle section over a modified cross-country course. There may be some show jumps on the cross-country if the siting is appropriate, i.e. after a bank when a horse is collected and in a frame. There is no timing because of the complexity of timing two combined phases. In practice the jumping penalties sort out the riders. Approximately five minutes is scheduled for each competitor.

| Level | Distance | Maximum height | Jumping efforts |
| --- | --- | --- | --- |
| Pre-Training | 1600m | 3ft 0in | 18–20 |
| Training | 1800m | 3ft 3in | 20–22 |
| Novice (UK) | 2000m | 3ft 6in | 21–24 |
| Preliminary | 2000m | 3ft 7in | 21–24 |

## Scoring

| | |
|---|---|
| Knockdown | 10 points |
| 1st refusal | 20 points |
| 2nd refusal at same fence | 40 points |
| 3rd refusal at same fence | Elimination |
| Fall of horse or rider | Elimination |
| 5 refusals on whole course | Elimination |

Combinations lettered AB, ABC or ABCD will be judged as per show jumping rules, i.e. if B is refused then A must be jumped on second presentation.

Circles on course will be judged as refusals.

Good points earned from dressage will be added to good points retained in jumping, and this determines the placings in each division. Ties are decided by the better score in the jumping round; if still tied, then by the better score in the 'general impression' section of the dressage test.

# Appendix B

## Horse Trials Organiser's Master Plan

*by kind permission of Russell Smith, Checkmate Horse Trials*

Comparisons have been made between organising a horse trials and an amphibious landing. The complexity of co-ordinating the different phases, the importance of exact timing and being prepared for the unexpected, are at the heart of running a successful show. A flowchart is not just a planning guide, but gives a quick visual reference to every facet of the competition at every moment of the day. The really well-thought-out charts, like the one overleaf, have a hidden subtext that enables the event controller to smoothly adjust the trim tabs in response to problems. Officials are aware that the show has lost the rudder and is drifting onto a lee shore; but by improvising and making minor adjustments the show and the announcer's dulcet commentary continue without skipping a beat.

- Competition schedule: Friday evening reception to Sunday evening.

- List of officials, staff and volunteers: telephone numbers and addresses.

- List of accommodation: location and telephone numbers for officials and key personnel.

- Summary of officials and staff requirements for each day:

- Official timetable: timetable for all personnel, Friday 6.30 am – Sunday 7.00 pm.

- Site and cross-country maps.

- Staff responsibilities and directives.

# DESIGN AND BUILD A CROSS-COUNTRY COURSE

## Checkmate Canadian Open, Intermediate & Preliminary Horse Trials – Saturday August 31
Russell Updated as of August 13

**Canadian Advanced Championships**
**Ontario Intermediate Championships**

### Check comments in Boxes below

|  | Sept 2001 | May 2002 | Sept Est. 2002 |
|---|---|---|---|
| Adv | 20 | 0 | 15 |
| Inter | 29 | 27 | 40 |
| Prelim | 46 | 45 | 50 |
| TOTAL | 95 | 72 | 105 |

**Notes Below:**
Advanced Dressage can use ring 1 for warmup
Intermediate can use Rings 3 & 4 for warmup after Prelim finishes
Prelim Stadium – see notes for Lise and Kathy re start time
Schedule tight if more than 50 Prelims and/or 15 Advanced
Check when numbers are known

### Schedule

Columns: Sat Aug 24 | Tues Aug 27 | Thurs Aug 29

**Breakfast Officials & Staff** — 6 7 (Breakfast)

**Prel Dressage A – Ring 3**
- SN Dressage – 15 | SN Dressage – 10 | Lch Kathy Slaney
- Warmup in grass ring in PT Start Field

**Prel Dressage B – Ring 4 nearest arena**
- SN Dressage – 15 | SN Dressage – 10 | Lunch Jennifer Klemm
- Warmup in grass ring in PT Start Field

**Preliminary Cross Country**
- 3 min starts | P&A | SN Brf MV | Prelim cross 50 | JJ Lunch Brf

**Preliminary Stadium**
- P&A | P&P | Chpk/prk | Stadium 50 | Kathy Slaney | RIB

**Cdn Open Adv Dressage Ring 2**
- 9 min ea | Dressage – 15 | SN | Lise Martin & Peta Christen

**Championship Warmup Ring 1** — Warmup Ring # 1

**Cdn Open Adv Stadium**
- A&I | | Stad 15 | Lunch | Lise Martin & Peta Christen

**Cdn Open Cross Country**
- A&A | | | 4 min starts | Brf | MV | Cross 15 | MV | RIB

**Intermediate Champ Dress – Ring 2**
- I&I | | | 9 min ea | Ch Dress 10 | SN | Ch Dress 10 | MV | Lise Martin & Peta Christen
- Warmup in Ring 3 & 4

**Intermediate Dressage – Ring 1**
- | | | 9 min ea | Dressage 10 | SN | Dressage 10 | Jennifer Klemm
- Warmup in Ring 3 & 4

**Intermediate Stadium**
- | | | | Engineer | Stadium 40 | Kathy Slaney

**Intermediate Cross Country**
- | | | 4 min starts | | MV | Cross 40 | RIB

**Volunteer Reception Arena Deck**
- 6 7 8 9 10 11 12 1 2 3 4 5 Vol Rec 6 7

Officials Dinner in Arena Second Floor at 7:30 pm. – 30 people

---

**KEY TO ABBREVIATIONS**
SN = snacks; Brf = breakfast; MV = move volunteers; RIB = ribbon or rosette presentation

# Appendix C

## Imperial and Metric Conversions

1 inch = 2.540 cm        1 cm = 0.393 inch
1 foot = 0.304 cm        1 m  = 3.281 feet
1 mile = 1.609 km        1 km = 0.621 miles

10in = 25.4cm    10cm = 3.93in

| WHEN YOU KNOW | MULTIPLY BY | TO FIND |
|---|---|---|
| inches | 2.54 | centimetres |
| centimetres | 0.3937 | inches |
| yards | 0.9 | metres |
| metres | 3.281 | feet |
| feet | 0.3048 | metres |
| miles | 1.609 | kilometres |
| kilometres | 0.6214 | miles |

# Appendix D

## Timber

The amount of timber required to build even a modest cross-country course can be a shock to organisers – five trees per jump, times twenty, is two fully loaded transport trucks. At first glance this can make a new course appear financially impossible. A closer look shows that jump builders are busier than ever and one of the reasons is that course construction operates on three levels. The first level is having a realistic budget and the knowledge to purchase the right materials at the right price. The next level is about using skill and ingenuity so more is done with less without sacrificing quality. The final level is how professional course builders procure timber, and this is by networking with local sawmills, arborists, demolition and recycling businesses and timber-supply merchants. It is critical to buy the right construction materials at the right price, and because there are so many variables and each region has its own challenges, it is strongly recommended that advice is sought from local course builders and designers. First, a primer on wood.

In broad terms there are two classes of trees – conifers, which generally keep their leaves all year round, and deciduous trees, which shed their leaves in the autumn. Conifers are called softwoods, and deciduous trees are known as hardwoods.

Carpenters further classify timber into sapwood and heartwood. The sapwood is the outer layer inside the bark and is the living part of a tree. Sapwood rots quickly outdoors. Heartwood makes up the bulk of a tree and is resistant to insects and rot.

The following is a brief list of some common jump-building material. Many of these trees are regarded as ornamental rather than commercial. Nevertheless, storms and urban sprawl bring down trees indiscriminately and it cannot be stressed enough that every log could become a jump.

## Softwoods

**Fir** *(Pinaceae family)* – many different varieties, all good jump potential but may only last five years outdoors. Will last longer if the bark is removed and the log is sanded and varnished.

**Hemlock** *(Tsuga canadenensis)* – lightweight, coarse-grained, water-resistant, one of the more durable softwoods. Reasonable rough-cut timber but tends to splinter easily.

**Juniper** *(Juniperus communis)* – tough rugged foliage is ideal for brush jumps.

**Larch** *(Larix family)* – Tamarack is a N. American variety. Long, straight, minimum taper and more durable than most softwood.

**Pine** *(Pinaceae family)* – soft pines (White Pine) rots quickly outdoors. Hard pines (e.g. Southern Yellow Pine) are more heavy, strong and durable.

**Redwood** *(Sequoia sempervirens)* – very durable and water resistant. Magnificent timber.

**Spruce** *(Pinaceae family)* – commercial lumber that is light, strong, and easy to work.

**White Cedar** *(Thuja occidentalis)* – one of the best species for course building. It lasts many years whether in or above the ground. Lightweight and easy to work with. Foliage is ideal for brush jumps.

**Western Red Cedar** *(Thuja plicata)* – magnificent timber for building, lasts many years, water-resistant.

## Hardwoods

**Ash** *(Fraxinus excelsior)* – commercial hardwood, strong, flexible. Not good in the ground, but tough and resilient above the ground.

**Beech** *(Fags sylvatica)* – related to oak and chestnut, hard and close-grained.

**Birch** *(Betulaceae family)* – silver birch is too beautiful to cut down, but when it begins to die off it is perfect for an ornamental jump at a water complex. Rots within three years.

**Cherry** *(Prunus family)* – Black Cherry does not last long outdoors unless the bark is removed. It is better to remove the bark, and sand and varnish rather than hide this rich timber beneath stain or toxic preservatives.

**Elm** *(Ulmus family)* – strong, hard, coarse grained. Will last many years if the bark is removed. Good underwater.

**Hickory** *(Carya family)* – tough, hard and heavy.

**Locust** *(Robinia pseudoacacia)* – quick-growing, hard, heavy, strong, very resistant to decay and shock. Lasts forever above or below the ground. Hard to work with but excellent timber.

**Maple** *(Acer family)* – two groups: the sugar or black maple is very hard, strong and heavy. Soft maples – sycamore, red, silver – are softer and decay faster.

**Oak** *(Quercus family)*– white oak heartwood is very hard and durable. Red oak, a N. American variety, is less durable.

**Poplar** *(Populus family)* – much maligned because it rots quickly outdoors. It is quick growing and short living. Mature trees do make substantial jumps; they just have to be replaced within five years. Lasts longer if the bark is removed.

**Sweet chestnut** *(Castanea family)* – high quality timber. Good for posts.

**Willow** *(Salix family)* – Weeping Willow is a wonderful decoration for water jumps. One of the easiest trees to propagate, just take a cutting and stick it in moist ground.

## New and Used Lumber

**Telephone poles** – ideal jump-building material. Strong, uniform and lasts many years. The best are made from Western Red Cedar and only have the butt creosoted.

**Railway sleepers or ties** – these have long been the mainstay for revetting banks and ditches. However, because of environmental concerns they are no longer recommended for use in watercourses.

**Pressure-treated timber** – popular because of high labour costs and the short life of many species outdoors. Downside is that pressure-treated timber is toxic, unaesthetic and its pale green colour can make a jump difficult to see. A sensible compromise is to use pressure-treated timber for posts and natural timber for rails.

**Rough-cut lumber** – this is unplaned timber from a sawmill. Course building requires timber that is stronger and of thicker dimensions than is normally used in the construction industry. Sawmills may not exist in more urban locales, but if they do they are worth visiting because they usually have the reputation of supplying quality timber at a reasonable price.

There are many ways of doing more with less, and these are discussed in Chapter 3. The first step in locating construction material is your local telephone or business directory. If that is not successful, then try calling course designers, builders or organisers. The finest and cheapest material comes from working with the one-man operations – the horse loggers, sawmill operators and the like – whose backfields can hide mountains of barn beams, sleepers and discarded telephone poles.

# APPENDIX E

## Fence by Fence Materials List

There are many variables that affect the timber requirements for building jumps. Design and construction skills, dimension of the lumber and the size of the jump all influence the amount of materials required. This list is given as a guide and is perhaps most useful as a reference for planning and working out a budget. Many jumps require short pieces of timber; for the sake of simplicity, I have rounded these out to the nearest 8ft (2.4m) post. It is important to refer to the text when making a materials list, as cheaper alternatives are described. Rope, nails and wire should be purchased in bulk and these requirements are not included here.

### Ascending rails
3 logs, 8in–10in (20cm–25cm) diameter     16ft–18ft (4.8m–5.4m) long
3 posts, 8in (20cm) diameter     8ft (2.4m) long

### Oxer
4 logs, 10in (25cm) diameter     16ft–18ft (4.8m–5.4m) long
6 posts, 8in (20cm) diameter     8ft (2.4m) long

### Table
4 logs, 10in (25cm) diameter     16ft–18ft (4.8m–5.4m) long
6 posts, 8in (20cm) diameter     8ft (2.4m) long
12 planks, 2in x 6in (5cm x 15cm)     12ft (3.6m) long

APPENDIX E | **FENCE BY FENCE MATERIALS LIST**

## Farm shelter

| | |
|---|---|
| 3 logs, 10in (25cm) diameter | 16ft–18ft (4.8m–5.4m) long |
| 12 posts, 8in (20cm) diameter | 7ft (2.1m) long |
| 12–18 planks, 2in x 6in (5cm x 15cm) | 12ft (3.6m) long |

## Steeplechase

| | |
|---|---|
| 3 logs, 10in (25cm) diameter | 16ft–18ft (4.8m–5.4m) long |
| 4 posts, 8in (20cm) diameter | 6ft (1.8m) long |
| 1 full wagon-load brush (minimum) | |

## Flower box

| | |
|---|---|
| 7 logs, 10in (25cm) diameter | 16ft–18ft (4.8m–5.4m) long |
| 6 logs, 10in (25cm) diameter | 4ft (1.2m) long |

## Sharks' teeth

| | |
|---|---|
| 1 log, 10in (25cm) diameter | 16ft–18ft (4.8m–5.4m) long |
| 3 posts, 8in (20cm) diameter | 8ft (2.4m) long |
| 8 planks, 2in x 6in (5cm x 15cm) | 12ft (3.6m) long |
| 4 half-rounds, 10in (25cm) diameter | 6ft (1.8m) long |

## Cordwood

| | |
|---|---|
| 3 logs, 8in–10in (20cm–25cm) diameter | 16ft–18ft (4.8m–5.4m) long |
| 4 posts, 8in (20cm) diameter | 8ft (2.4m) long |
| 2 logs, 4–6in (10–15cm) diameter | 16ft (4.8m) long |
| Stack of logs approx. 4ft x 4ft x 16ft (1.2m x 1.2m x 4.8m) | |

## Log cabin

| | |
|---|---|
| 7 logs, 10in (25cm) diameter | 16ft–18ft (4.8m–5.4m) long |
| 4 logs, 10in (25cm) diameter | 12ft (3.6m) long |
| 12–14 planks, 2in x 6in (5cm x 15cm) | 12ft (3.6m) long |

## Stone wall with one top rail

| | |
|---|---|
| 1 log, 10in (25cm) diameter | 16ft–18ft (4.8m–5.4m) long |
| 2 posts, 8in (20cm) diameter | 8ft (2.4m) long |
| 10–12 cubic yards/metres of fieldstone | |

### Corner

| | |
|---|---|
| 4 logs, 10in (25cm) diameter | 10ft (3m) long |
| 6 posts, 8in (20cm) diameter | 8ft (2.4m) long |
| 6 planks, 2in x 6in (5cm x 15cm) | 12ft (3.6m) long |

### Ditch

| | |
|---|---|
| 16–20 railway sleepers (ties) | 8ft (2.4m) long |
| *or* 10 pressure-treated 6in x 6in (15cm x 15cm) | 16ft (4.8m) long |
| 3 steel fence posts | 7ft (2.1m) long |
| 3 posts, 8in (20cm) diameter | 6ft (1.8m) long |

### Trakehner

*The same materials for a ditch plus:*

| | |
|---|---|
| 1 log, 16in (40cm) diameter | 16ft–18ft (4.8m–5.4m) long |
| 1 log, 12in (30cm) diameter | 16ft–18ft (4.8m–5.4m) long |
| 8 posts, 8in–10in (20cm–25cm) diameter | 8ft (2.4m) long |

### Normandy bank

| | |
|---|---|
| 20 pressure-treated 6in x 6in (15cm x 15cm) | 18ft (5.4m) long (one stride) |
| *or* 32 railway sleepers | 8ft (2.4m) long |
| 8 posts, 8in (20cm) diameter | 6ft (1.8m) long |
| 3 logs, 8in (20cm) diameter | 18ft (5.4m) long |
| 5 steel fence posts | 7ft (2.1m) long |

### Triple steps

| | |
|---|---|
| 15 pressure-treated 6in x 6in (15cm x 15cm) | 16ft (4.8m) long |
| *or* 24 railway sleepers | 8ft (2.4m) long |
| 5 posts, 8in (20cm) diameter | 6ft (1.8m) long |
| 5 steel fence posts | 7ft (2.1m) long |

## NOTE

In practice the course designer explains the concept of a jump to the builder, who will then use his or her ingenuity and the realities of the project to construct the fence. Consequently it is critical that the designer, builder and organiser are in agreement with all the details of the construction. This list serves as a starting point in that discussion.

# Index

access, vehicular 13, 173
accidents 172–4
apron 177
arrowhead 25

banks 111–12
    footing 111, 124
    Irish 115–16
    location 119
    multi-tiered 117–19
    Normandy 112–15, 190
    pony club course 156–7
    striding 35, 36, 114
black flag rule 25, 177
boulders, moving 146
bounce 35, 36
bridge building 170
brush jumps 24
    construction 67–8
    materials 20, 66–7
    pony club course 154
bulldozer 126, 147

camber 13, 177
chainsaw 59, 137
    carving 147
    maintenance 148
    ripping logs 139
    safety 138
coffins 108–10
combinations
    design 95–6, 97
    downhill 27
    striding 35, 36
    see also types of combination fence
control, encouraging 15–16
corduroy road 33, 168
cordwoods 74–6
    construction 75–6
    materials 75, 189
    offset 108

corners 25, 83
    construction 84–5
    double 105–6
    materials 83, 190
cost-effectiveness 18–21, 149, 152
course builder
    qualities of 9
    safety education 50
    stress 147–8
course design 14–17
    cost-effectiveness 18–21, 149, 152
    level of difficulty 14–15
    pony club course 158
    poor 18–19, 22–8
    principles 17
course layout 11, 12, 119
course walking 158–9
crisis management 173–4
crusher dust 30
crusher-run 30, 129, 177

digging bar 139
distance, of course 15
ditches 25, 86
    construction methods 87–90
    drainage 168–9
    materials 87, 190
    pony club course 153–4
    striding 35, 36
    see also coffins; trakehner
donors 151–2
dovetail joins 78, 79
dovetail notches 142
downhill fences 27, 102
dowsing 131
drainage 33, 149, 168–70
drop fences 26, 93–4

earthworms 29, 32

education, of rider 15–16, 95
equestrian sport, changes in 160
equipment 136, 137–9, 148–9
excavations, use of 19, 114

falling, art of 175–6
falls 172–4
farm pen 98, 99
farm shelter 60
    construction 46, 61–3
    materials 61, 189
filler fences 16
final fences 16
financing of events 151–2
first fences 15
flower-box
    construction 43–4
    materials 43, 45, 189
    pony club course 157–8
    with top rail 44–6
flowers, use of 157, 158
footing 11, 13, 23, 29–33
    banks and steps 111, 124
    repairing 32–3
    water jumps 25, 26, 126–7, 129, 135
    wet ground 33

garden frame 69–71
geotextile membrane 30–1, 126–7, 134, 135, 177
    alternatives to 30, 149
gravel 32–3, 129
    types of 30, 177, 178
ground lines 24
ground rails, fastening 140

hillside rails 103
hillsides 167–70
hog's back 153
holes, filling 32

horse trials, organiser's master plan 181–2
hunter trials 161–2

illusions, optical 27
Irish bank 115–16

JCBs 126, 131
jump judges, pony club 159

lakes 134
log cabin 76–9, 189
log jumps 153, 155, 158
logging chains 147
logs
    joining notches 140–2
    moving heavy 142–4, 147
    ripping 139, 177–8
loose horses 172

machinery 138, 148–9
manure, use of 29, 32, 33, 149
master plan, horse trials organisation 181–2
materials
    fence by fence list 188–90
    sourcing 19–20, 152
    timber types 184–5
measures 183
membrane
    geotextile 30–1, 126–7, 134, 135, 149, 177
    waterproof 131–4
metric conversions 183
multiple-use jumps 20, 98, 99

nails 149–50
Normandy bank 112–15, 190
notches 140–2

offset rails 106–8

191

# INDEX

options 16
organiser 19
   master plan 181–2
oxer
   materials and construction 55–7, 188
   portable fence 46–8

parallel rails 27
   materials and construction 55–7
   portable 46–8
park bench 155
peavey 143, 177
pit-run gravel 30, 129, 177
ponds 134
pony club courses
   design 158
   fence building 153–8
   jump judges 159
   learning how to walk 158–9
   sponsorship 151–2
   work parties 152–3
portable fences 37–8, 105
   ascending rails 38–9, 155
   building tips 48–9
   flower box 42–6
   parallel rails/oxer 46–8
   roll top 40–2
post holes 138–9
   awkward/in water 145–6, 170
post and rails 50–4
   construction methods 51–4
   materials 188
   portable ascending 38–9, 155
   *see also* parallel rails
posts, setting 54, 139
   angled 57
publicity, advance 163–4
pumps 130–1

quarry combinations 103–5
questions 15–16, 96, 97

rails
   ascending 38–9, 50–4, 155
   hillside 103
   offset 106–8
   roping 14, 140
   *see also* post and rails
railway sleepers (ties) 142, 186
ramp 156
revetting 142, 177
   backfilling 114–15
   banks and steps 112, 113, 116, 124
   water jumps 132, 133, 135
rider education 15–16, 158–9
rip-rap 30, 114, 178
ripping (logs) 139, 177–8
risk 171
risk assessment 172, 173
road building 33, 167–8
road crossing 100
roll top (portable) 40–2
roping 140, 141
rules 25, 163–4, 177

saddle notch 140–2
safety 22–3, 28, 171–4
   education 50
   rules 164
scalpings 30, 178
screenings 30, 129, 178
sharks' teeth 71–4
   construction 73–4
   materials 72–3, 189
short course eventing 160–1, 179–80
site, walking 13, 15
site plan 11, 12
ski ramp 63–5
slopes 24, 27, 102
   striding 34, 36

slopes *cont.*
   water jumps 125–6
sponsors 151–2
spread fences 26–7
standards, of course 14–15, 163–4
standards of care 174
steeplechase fence 67–8, 189
steps 120–4
   footing 124
   materials 190
   striding 35, 36
   triple 123–4
stone dust 129
stone walls 80–2
   construction 81–2
   materials 80–1, 189
   pony club course 154
streams 134
stress, course builder's 147–8
striding 34–6, 178
   measuring 35
   standard distances 35
   variables affecting 36
stunt riders 175, 176
sunken road 100–3

table
   construction 46, 58–9
   design 23–4
   materials 58, 188
tarpaulins 149
team chases 162–3
telegraph poles 142, 186
   moving 142–4
timber 184–5
   dimensions 23
   moving heavy 142–4, 147
   sources 20, 152, 186–7
   types 185–6
toe-nailing 142
tools 136, 137–9
topsoil 149

track surface
   camber 13, 177
   *see also* footing
tractor 138, 142
training centre courses 165–6
trakehner 16, 91
   construction 92–3
   materials 91–2, 190
transit 125, 135
tree felling 144–5
turf, care of 29, 31–2
turns 13
tyre jumps 154, 156

vehicles
   access to fences 13, 173
   moving stuck 146–7
vertical fences 23, 24
vision, horse's 27
volunteers 20–1, 152–3

warm-up rings, safety 172–3
washed gravel 178
water jumps
   design and costs 19, 25–6, 126–7, 129–31
   filling 130–1
   footing 25, 26, 126–7, 129, 135
   guard rails 170
   jumps before 27, 96
   jumps into 26, 94
   location 125–6
   post holes 145–6, 170
   tips for 134–5
   use of waterproof liner 131–4
weather 16, 173
wet ground 33, 167–70
woodland 13, 32
woodshavings manure 32, 33, 149
work parties 20–1, 152–3